# girls just wanna have funds

# girls just wanna have funds

## a feminist guide to investing

Emma Due Bitz
Camilla Falkenberg
Anna-Sophie Hartvigsen

# CONTENTS

# Don't think investing sounds interesting? No problem. We're not here to have fun; we're here to make money and claim our power.

# Note to the reader

This book is written primarily with women and nonbinary people in mind, but we invite anyone who supports the mission of closing the financial gender gap to read it and learn from it...

For the ones who've been left out of the narrative.

For the ones who've been told
they can't or shouldn't.

For the ones who've wanted something more.

It's time to shift the tides of power and claim our rightful seat at the table. We welcome anyone and everyone to take charge of their financial future in the name of a new status quo.

This book is for you. You deserve to be heard.

# Money
# is
# power

Women are now entering higher education in record numbers. They are climbing the corporate ladder, running for political office, pushing against the glass ceiling, and pursuing power as never before. However, there is one area yet to be addressed: money.

Money equals power and opportunity. It brings you the essentials in life—food, shelter, clothing and education—but it can also do so much more than that; it can buy you the freedom to do what you've always wanted. Take that trip. Make music. Build a company. Get your kids off to a good start. Perhaps even use it to do your bit to make the world a better place.

But although money is an essential element of life, it is something that women and marginalized communities have historically been excluded from earning and managing. As a result, there's not a single country in the world where men and women are financially equal. In fact, the World Economic Forum estimates that it will take 257 years to close the financial gender gap. This effectively means that, today, no woman will live long enough to experience a world in which she has the same level of freedom and opportunity as her male peers. Let's get this straight: Nothing bad happens when women

*There are 195 countries in the world. Not a single one has achieved financial gender equality.*

have more money. In fact, quite the opposite—it benefits individuals, companies, and society as a whole when women are able to spend and invest. A McKinsey & Company study from 2015 found that if women were to participate in the economy on equal terms to men, they could add as much as the combined size of the economies of the United States and China today to the world's GDP. How remarkable is that?

Still, the discussion around money is sensitive, tainted with emotions, values and personal beliefs held by ourselves and instilled in us by the generations before us. In this book, we'll do our best to outline the current state of financial equality—and what you can do to improve it for women of our generation and for those to come.

We don't have to sit around and wait for change to happen. There are many ways by which we can take action ourselves, and our aim with this book is to offer you concrete advice on what you can do to optimize your own financial situation and to help everyone around you achieve the same success.

*Because one thing is certain. Money is power—and women need more of both.*

# Gender stereotypes kill dreams

Gender stereotyping is still alive and well in the twenty-first century. From the moment babies are born, their assigned sex immediately begins to shape how they will be treated, what opportunities they will receive, and how they will behave according to dominant gender stereotypes in their society. The most significant influence on gender role development occurs within the family setting, with parents modelling and passing on to their children their own beliefs about gender. You may recognize this trend from your own childhood. For example, did your parents teach you how to manage money? Did they participate equally in all of your family's financial decision-making? In the UK today, 68% of girls feel held back by harmful gender stereotypes.

# Is financial inequality just a gender issue?

It would be easy to make a case about men versus women, but when talking about financial gender inequality we need to consider factors *beyond* gender, too. "Women" are not a homogenous group, and different categories of people have different experiences. As formulated by Kimberlé Crenshaw, an American law professor and the woman who coined the term *Intersectional feminism*: "All inequality is not created equal."

Simply put, this means that different types of discrimination, such as gender, race, class, and sexuality, overlap, creating compounding experiences of discrimination. We can't talk about one without recognizing the existence and impact of others. For example, Black, Asian, and minority ethnic women experience sexism differently from white women in a society that affords privilege to whiteness. Trans women don't have the privilege of cisgender women; people with disabilities are not enabled to participate in work to the same extent as able-bodied citizens; migrants are often excluded from the very financial systems that we want to help you understand.

Therefore, looking at the current state of financial inequality isn't enough to change attitudes; we also need to recognize the historical context of the issue. Decades of systemic discrimination have created deep inequities that disadvantage some people in society from the very beginning, and this extends across generations. This is especially important when we are talking about money, as we know that women have historically been excluded from earning, saving, and managing it—especially women and girls of color.

Another factor that significantly impacts your relationship with money is your current life situation. Do you have a job? Are you in a relationship? How is your health? How is your financial health? We all have different starting points when it comes to investing, which is why we encourage everyone to read this book with their own experience in mind.

*It's not just about money. It's about freedom, independence, and the ability to live life on your own terms.*

# Parents are more likely to teach their daughters about the importance of saving while educating their sons about building wealth.

# The current state of financial inequality

When it comes to money, we like to think that men and women will receive the same opportunities if they put in the same amount of work and dedication. But the uncomfortable truth is that women face a large number of discriminatory barriers, some of which are so deeply ingrained in society that many are blind to them or even deny their existence. For starters, women earn less than men—even when they are doing the same jobs.

In developed countries, women in higher education outnumber men. They achieve better academic results and make better leaders once they enter the workforce. However, they still earn less, are poorly represented in politics, and are less likely to join the top ranks in business or become entrepreneurs.

# THE GENDER WAGE GAP

The wage gap, combined with factors such as women being more likely to live longer and more likely to take a career break or choose part-time work, can have a major impact on a woman's financial situation over her lifetime. For example, a 10% pay gap alone can lead to approximately 38% less wealth by the age of 65. Could women change this themselves? Probably not, because even when women ask for a raise, they are less likely to get it and more likely to be viewed as greedy and demanding.

These facts refer to women who are in paid work but, globally, 42% of women aren't in the paid workforce because they are doing unpaid, largely invisible work at home. Does this work have value? Very much so. In fact, a study into unpaid labor conducted by PwC found that, in the US alone, the value of the unpaid economy was $565 billion—worth around a third of the entire economy—and the vast majority of this is attributed to childcare.

So this concerns the gender pay gap, but we also have to consider the gender *wealth* gap.

# THE GENDER WEALTH GAP

While the pay gap refers to compensation, the wealth gap is the overall difference in net worth between men and women, which is affected by a lot of things besides pay.

The systemic barriers for women go far beyond the job market. For example, women have more student loans, are denied mortgages more frequently, and when they are granted loans they are charged higher interest rates on them. They also pay more for housing investments and receive lower-quality financial advice. Research finds that women are much more likely to be advised to save, whereas men are advised to invest. And according to the World Economic Forum, these inequalities start early—studies show that young girls consistently get less pocket money than young boys and are expected to do more chores around the home.

Throughout our lives, these stereotypes around women and money are reinforced by the education system, by financial institutions, and even in relationships—parents are more likely to teach their daughters about the importance of saving while educating their sons about building wealth. At every step of our lives, from our earliest days, girls and women are being excluded from learning, earning, saving, and investing.

*Globally, men own 50% more wealth than women.*

# Experiencing discrimination through gender transition

Until the age of 49, Caroline Farberger was living as Carl, a high-powered executive of the Swedish insurance company ICA, who believed gender inequality was a rational choice with rational consequences. It wasn't until transitioning as a woman in 2017 and becoming Sweden's first transgender CEO that Caroline was confronted with the whole picture of what it means to be a woman.

Opening up about her own previous biases, Caroline shares how her transition impacted her views on gender equality, made her more informed about a woman's perspective, and how she is empowered to join the movement for change.

**Getting clear on gender equality:**
When I lived as a man, I thought I knew it all when it came to gender equality. I observed the differences, but I thought there were rational justifications simply because women weren't as confident as men. It only took me a few months of living as a woman to understand that I had totally misunderstood it, because women really started to talk to me about their experiences.

**Building inclusivity:** After coming out, a female colleague told me that as a man, my leadership team was one of the most difficult they experienced. They told me I was dominating, that I started the meetings by stating my opinion and what the result should be, and that I let the other men who thought like me talk. I thought that was an efficient way of running the business: come to quick decisions and move on. Now I view that as a dangerous thing, because the quicker you make a decision without getting the other perspective, the more likely it is you're taking things in completely the wrong direction. So now I try to encourage different perspectives and refrain from influencing how people around me should think.

**The importance of education:**
Educate yourself around biases and privileges. When I was a man, I was privileged. To belong to a societal "norm"—whether it's due to gender, skin color, or another aspect—is a privilege, because most social structures around you are built for those in that position. If you are born into a marginalized category, things are more difficult. That's just how daily life works. But you can change this—you can share your privilege by inviting others to talk in meetings or influence a decision.

**It is *not* a man's world:** We need less gender-stereotypical behavior and more strong role models. We must educate men on seeing and acknowledging the value of people who are different, and we must resist the temptation to mimic normative behaviors to fit in. Women are disadvantaged when it comes to both confidence and financial matters. I know it's easier said than done, but we all have a responsibility to change the status quo—especially those with greater privilege. Many female networks almost teach women to behave like men. I don't subscribe to that theory; by doing that, all you do is permanently allow men to play a home game and tell women that this is a man's place—that women should learn how to play an away game every day for the rest of their career. Rather, we should have a joint playing field where everyone can truly be themselves.

# Three major questions we're asked about financial inequality

**1**

### Are women less qualified?
No – in fact, the opposite is true; women in developed countries are more educated than men, but they don't receive the same financial remuneration or status for the work they do. And yet, when it comes to investing, women in developed countries achieve better financial returns when they do invest.

**2**

### Are things improving?
Not significantly. Even though we *are* talking more about the topic than ever before, progress in this area has ground to a near halt. Globally, women's participation in the workforce has stagnated for two decades, while women's income share hasn't changed much in the past 30 years.

**3**

### Have we acknowledged the problem?
In the US, only 12% of men think women have fewer opportunities for advancing in their career. In Europe the numbers are similar, with more than one-third of Europeans believing that men are more ambitious than women, and almost seven in ten respondents thinking women are more likely than men to make decisions based on their emotions.

# Zooming in

## THE GENDER INVESTMENT GAP

This depressing news continues, because when it comes to investing, women are falling behind here, too. Female investors are still a minority, and in the financial industry, women are a rare sight in executive positions.

The fact that women are underrepresented in financial markets inevitably raises the question: "Are men better investors?" The answer to this is a clear-cut "no." That's not just our experience from running one of the world's largest investment communities for women—we are backed up on this by several studies that have concluded that women investing in stocks are better at it than men.

So that's what this book is all about. We're going to help women to get onto the investment ladder and take control of their financial future. We've got this—we've just got to get started.

# FIRST...

# PREPARE

# 1

# Invest in you

If you have picked up this book with aspirations of improving your financial future, that's great; our intention is to help you do just that. But before we get started, it's important that you understand your own money story— that you are aware of the role your existing beliefs and your attitudes toward money have in shaping your current financial behavior.

Our money habits in adulthood can feel sticky and hard to change because they are formed very early in life and have become our way of doing things. It is our parents who are often our first teachers and also our most lasting examples of how to handle our finances. If our earliest memories of money management were of witnessing our parents scraping by and struggling to make ends meet, that is likely to have an impact on our attitudes toward money as we grow up.

A study from the American Academy of Pediatrics found a correlation between the amount of total debt a family had and the poor social and emotional well-being of their children.

You might find this information a bit discouraging, but don't; just because your family's financial situation growing up was less than ideal, that doesn't mean you can't become financially successful yourself. The important thing is to be mindful of the things we pick up on as children, so that we can prevent these dictating how we then manage our money as adults.

*Financial confidence empowers you to take charge of your financial future.*

# Find financial confidence

Confidence counts for so much in life; it helps you get the dream job you want, take on new challenges, and navigate the obstacles life can throw at you. Financial confidence is an important part of this; it helps you take control of your money and gives you a much stronger chance of fulfilling the goals that matter to you. It's important to understand that financial empowerment and women's empowerment go hand in hand; this is a message we will repeat unashamedly—and we want you to hold on to this right through this book and beyond!

We know that women have a hard time talking about money and power. For example, 80% of women hold back from discussing money with family and friends, yet 92% of women want to learn more about financial planning, according to a survey by Fidelity Investments. Research shows that women tend to be less financially confident than men, and yet we know that they outperform their male counterparts when it comes to investments and savings.

But what is financial confidence? According to Olga Miler, Managing Director at UBS Wealth Management, financial confidence has three aspects:

1. **Awareness** of how money can be a tool for helping you reach your goals in both the short and long run.
2. **Financial literacy** and practical knowledge of economic and financial topics that are relevant to your decisions.
3. **Trust** and knowing where to turn for help.

This is all well and good, you might be thinking, but how do we get there? The route to financial confidence isn't always straight, but we've gathered together four steps to try to make the journey a little easier and reduce the bumps in the road.

### 1 Build your money skills

Your money skills are built in two ways: learning and doing. Just by reading this book, you're already well underway with the first one. Understanding the basics of money is key to having confidence in managing it; if you learn the lingo, the topic will be much more approachable and you'll feel more comfortable navigating conversations and asking questions. But having the knowledge isn't enough, you also need to be willing and able to take action. Being perfect is not the goal, getting started is.

### 2 Reclaim your financial identity

We all do it; we tell ourselves stories about who we are and what we're good at. In many ways, these stories define us, both to ourselves and to the world around us. If you're insecure about money management, it's time to distance yourself from the "I'm rubbish with money" persona. By taking small steps toward owning your financial identity, you can take control of the stories you are telling yourself. This is important, because even small edits to your personal narrative can have a big impact on your life.

### 3 Set a financial goal

Setting and reaching a financial goal can be a huge confidence booster—whether it's paying off debt, starting a F*** U Fund (see page 44) or even saving $20 per month. Holding yourself accountable and having a successful experience with your finances will make it much easier for you to confidently set the next goal and plan for the future.

### 4 Protect your money and avoid lifestyle creep

Money is precious and should be treated as such. How long did you work to make it? Does what you're spending it on add value to you or take you closer to your goals?

A common pitfall is lifestyle creep, which happens when you increase your spending as your income grows, rather than saving more of it. This often happens for one of three reasons: failing to have a plan for your additional income; neglecting to plan for the future; or comparing yourself to others. The comparison trap is particularly dangerous. Be warned: There are financial unknowns happening behind the scenes for every person—they may be deeply in debt or have got their money through inheritance rather than earning it. The point is, you never *really* know what others can truly afford or why they can afford it, so don't get caught up in trying to keep up with the neighbors.

# IF YOU FALL DOWN, GET BACK UP

You will discover a few roadblocks along your journey to financial confidence. For example, you might find yourself missing a financial goal or losing money to a bad investment. That's normal. Confidence is built over time and trial; if you suffer a setback, commit to your goal and build courage so you can continue to take action and positively move forward

There's an irony to becoming confident: Some types of confidence can only be gained through experience. When you're wrong about something or fail at something, don't lose confidence in yourself; instead, reject that particular belief or your particular method. When it comes to finances, the best approach for building confidence is to ask questions about what you don't know, get smarter, then share that knowledge with others.

So let's all get comfortable with being a little uncomfortable and be more confident talking about money, power, and finances. Remember, as you grow your financial confidence, you get closer to financial freedom.

# Make a plan for financial success

We all have goals we want to achieve—whether that's buying our dream house, visiting exotic places, or retiring early. What we often forget is that most of our goals are directly impacted by our financial situation—and wishful thinking alone won't get us there. Therefore, the first step toward reaching your goals is taking control of your finances, so you can make sure that your bank account matches your dreams.

By setting goals for yourself, you can track your progress—and there's nothing like checking off a goal as you achieve it to get you excited about what you can accomplish next. Remember, it's never too late to start, no matter what your age (see pages 51–55), and financial goals are often a work in progress rather than a fixed result.

So, let's talk about how to set yourself financial goals—and stick to them!

*Financial goals are often a work in progress rather than a fixed result.*

# THE GOLDEN RULES OF SETTING GOALS

Before you start defining your money goals, there is one thing to keep in mind: Your goals should be SMART. That means: Specific, Measurable, Achievable, Realistic, and Time-bound.

### Specific
It can be tempting to set a goal such as "improve my finances," but what does that mean? When you look back in a year to see if you have achieved it, how will you be able to tell? So be specific in your goal—set it out clearly.

### Measurable
If you can't measure your progress, how will you gauge it and therefore keep yourself motivated and moving forward with every success? To do this you need to clearly state what you want to achieve in terms that can be measured. For example, decide: I want to save $5,000

### Achievable
If your money goal is not something you can work toward or potentially achieve, what's the point? Write down what you need to do each week in order to reach that ultimate goal, and be realistic about what is possible.

### Realistic
In the same vein as achievable, don't set yourself up for failure by setting wild goals you know you won't be able to achieve. It's important to find a balance, where your goals are both challenging and realistic, so be honest with yourself about what obstacles you can overcome and what you can manage—but don't undersell yourself!

### Time-bound

Finally, your goals should have a deadline. Make sure you set a specific time by which a certain goal needs to be achieved, so you can break down your progress into quarterly, monthly and weekly goals in the lead-up to that date.

When you have decided on two to five goals, we suggest you write them down. There is something magic about putting pen to paper and writing down what you want to accomplish. It gives your goals life, it serves as a reminder to you, and they'll become even more real when you see them on paper.

# WHAT'S NEXT?

Once you have set out your goals, it's time to look at each one individually and make a schedule. Let's say your goal is to save $5,000 over the next 12 months; if you break this down, this means you'll need to save $416 a month, or $104 a week.

For each of your goals, divide them into chunks and start tracking them daily, weekly, monthly, or quarterly. Again, write this down on paper or set up a spreadsheet.

Finally, you will need to make a schedule of actions; this could include things like:

- Updating your budget to reflect your new goals.
- Calling your bank to open a dedicated savings account, then setting up automatic transfers into it either weekly or monthly.

# Try to anticipate the challenges ahead

Whether you want to have a family, need to care for a loved one, or just fancy stepping out of the conventional world of work for a little while, there might come a time when you want to take a career break. However, remember that doing so could impact your long-term financial picture.

Women may be more likely to take a career break, but you can still stay on track of your financial goals by planning for the long-term. Hope Taitz, CEO at ELY Capital, advises that you: "Look at your overall financial picture rather than just your current snapshot – don't think about only what you're earning at age 30 when you may be having kids, but how your salary will grow over time."

If you choose to take a career break and feel you have any spare time while doing so, think about how you can stay relevant to your industry or profession. Perhaps you could get involved in related projects, in volunteering, or just make sure you stay updated on industry movements? Anything like this will keep you in the loop and help your CV to stay active and up to date if/when you decide to opt back in.

# Putting your goals into action

The hard work starts once you've decided on your goals, because now it's time to actually reach them! As with any journey, you will experience failures and setbacks along the way, which can make you lose motivation on occasion and, unfortunately, because of this many people give up on their goals before they even have a chance to make real progress.

But there's no reason why achieving your financial goals has to be difficult; people who are successful in this practice the following:

## 1 Focus on your schedule of actions, not the goal deadline

Sometimes focusing on a deadline can make it seem as if what you want to accomplish is so far away that you have plenty of time to get things done "later" and so you put them off, but then all of a sudden that deadline is so close that it's too late to do anything. When you focus on your staggered schedule of actions for the big goals, you are more likely to do what's required to accomplish your goals as a result of your consistent actions, bringing you steadily closer to the end result.

## Reward yourself along the way

Your financial goals might be established for the long term, and if you're a highly motivated person it's easy to get frustrated if you don't see change overnight. So instead of chasing one long-term goal, aim for steady change a little at a time, with rewards built in, rather than trying to radically overhaul your entire life in a bid to achieve the impossible. So don't cut spending on *all* your favorite things, set aside a portion of your budget to devote to small treats now and then, which you can use as a reward if at the end of the month you've stuck to your financial goals. Having a reward system helps you avoid splurging if you're getting frustrated during a rough patch in your journey. It also makes saving more rewarding, rather than a means of self-punishment for any previous financial mistakes you feel you have made.

## Surround yourself with like-minded people

If you are setting out to save a specific amount of money or pay off a certain amount of debt, it's best to be around people with a similar mindset. Surrounding yourself with supportive, money-savvy people is one of the best ways to stay motivated; they can keep you accountable for your financial goals and cheer you on along the way rather than pressure you into spending money that you are looking to save. Don't be afraid to talk about your plans, as once you start articulating your financial goals, you'll be surprised at how many people who are already in your network are looking to achieve the same things.

### Keep educating yourself

When it comes to efficient money management, there's a lot of learning by doing. However, educating yourself on the topic can help you to get ahead, because learning from the mistakes that others have made is much more beneficial than having to learn the hard way. Also, you might pick up some tips and tricks that can help you accelerate your own journey!

There are multiple ways to educate yourself on the topic of personal finance; depending on your preferred way of learning you can try podcasts, books, YouTube videos, blogs, and more. When choosing your source of education, always remember to be critical of it. Are they trying to sell you something? Do they have a hidden agenda? Finding impartial financial advice can be difficult, so you always need to be wary of a source that seems to be promoting specific financial products.

### Start small

You've probably heard of the snowball effect, which is normally used for paying off debt (see page 46). The snowball effect suggests that although it may make sense to pay off your largest debts first, starting with the smallest ones instead is great for your psyche because you get to celebrate the small wins much faster than if you started with your highest balances. This in turn will keep you motivated and excited to go after your bigger financial goals.

# Coming to grips with your finances

In order to master money, you must first manage money. Whether you are dreaming of retiring early, buying a house, or just beginning to invest, taking control of your personal finances is the starting point.

This is important for everyone, regardless of your income level or family situation. Being in control of your finances will allow you to navigate your life freely when unforeseen events occur, or even when you just want to make changes to it. This is especially important for women, who still tend to take the back seat on long-term financial decisions. The good news? Taking control of your money starts with something as simple as a budget.

It's not exactly a sexy topic—agreed—but creating a budget should always be the first step on your financial journey. The purpose of a budget is **not** to punish yourself for enjoying life and spending money on things you care about, rather, it's about creating an overview of your financial situation and making sure you are spending the way you intend to. Also, keep in mind that we all start somewhere and our budget is not fixed; it can and should be altered whenever your financial situation changes.

## Did you know?

If you invested $2,050 when your child is born, and not a penny more, and that money saw a 10% annual rate of return, your child could be a millionaire at 65.

# KNOW YOUR INCOME AND EXPENSES

Your income is often quite easy to grasp, as most of us don't have many sources for this—typically it looks something like paychecks, bonuses, or financial support from the government. However, on the other hand, it can be tricky to collate all of your expenses and get a clear picture of where exactly your money is going.

To get a grip on this, it's important to break down your spending. Expenses essentially come in two different variations: fixed or variable.

**Fixed expenses** are the type you can't avoid, whether you like it or not. These are paid on a regular basis—once a month, quarterly, or yearly. Examples of fixed expenses are mortgages, rent, transport, childcare, insurance, loans, etc.

**Variable expenses** are items of expenditure that you have a little more control over when it comes to budget; these include family activities, carry-out food, beauty products, and gifts.

**CARRIENE**

# "A positive money mindset is key."

If anyone understands the importance of shifting your money mindset, it's entrepreneur Carriene Rendbo, founder of I Love Natural Hair, a company that helps women embrace their wavy, curly, and Afro-textured hair. Through starting her own business in 2011, Carriene has learned to view money as a powerful tool that can work for you. In her continued march toward financial success, Carriene believes that "making small changes can make the biggest difference," so here are some of her tips on how to change your mindset to gain control over your finances.

**Ownership is important:** My mother always said that we kids should own a house, but I want to take it a step further with my children; I would like them to own a house, but also to own parts of companies through investing—I want that to be a normal conversation around our dinner table. I was very spontaneous with my money before I started investing, and I lived frivolously from paycheck to paycheck. I never thought about investing and I was very much a consumer rather than an owner.

**Be less afraid of money:** Before I had my own business, big numbers frightened me, and I was less likely to take risks. My mindset has changed since then, and I now see money as a powerful tool.

**Pay yourself first:** I truly believe the best investment is in yourself. Every time I get my salary, once I've paid my bills, I pay myself 20%, then I put 10% into a savings account and 10% into an investment account. It requires self-discipline, but doing that and sticking to it has been a game changer.

**Play the long game:** Consistency is key, even when it's not going well, and remembering to not get distracted from the end goal. I believe the successes I've had in my business and finances have definitely come from being consistent.

**Change your mindset:** I believe that it's when you change your view on money that you're able to attract more of it. That's because you see more opportunities to make it, rather than seeing it as something you could never achieve. I'm still on that journey.

# CREATE A WORKABLE BUDGET

The purpose of creating a budget is so that you can purposely control where your money goes rather than looking around and wondering where it all went. By following a budget you can also stay on track and work toward the money goals you have set for yourself.

There are many different budgeting tools and guidelines that are freely available. However, we like the 50/30/20 rule, because it takes both your present situation and "Future You" into account. The idea behind this is that you split your income into three categories:

50% Necessities       30% Fun       20% Future You

*Having a budget is telling your money where to go, rather than wondering where it went.*

## 50% for necessities

This includes expenses you *need* to pay for, such as housing, dentist bills, transportation, insurance, groceries, memberships, phone bills, internet, and minimum debt contributions. There's no way of avoiding these payments, so these should all be included in your budget.

## 30% for fun!

Although it might sound counterintuitive, the key to sticking to your budget is thinking about Present You and allowing yourself some fun. Whether it's a night out, going to a concert, a weekend trip, or something else you enjoy doing—do it! If you remove all the fun stuff you're definitely not going to stick to your budget.

## 20% for Future You

Your budget also needs to take care of Future You, meaning you can't spend all your money on fun and present necessities. That's why 20% of your income should go toward investing and saving. If you have debt with high interest rates (anything between 7 and 10%), you should focus on paying that off before you start to invest.

The 50/30/20 rule might not work for you, and that's okay—you can choose a different way to manage your money. However, make sure that whatever method of budgeting you decide on takes care of the Future You, because she deserves a good life!

And remember: If your financial situation changes substantially (if you ace a salary negotiation, for example) you should adjust your budget according to your new income. The same works for a less-positive change in circumstances, too! The point is to be flexible.

# The importance of a F*** U Fund

Through investments, you can take care of Future You and your financial goals for the future. Now, that's great, but you also need to take care of Present You, which is why you need an emergency savings account. We have named this the F*** U Fund.

Your F*** U Fund is money that sits in your bank account and is accessible at all times, which gives you the ultimate freedom of choice. If you are sick of your job and want to quit, or if you want to leave your partner or pursue a really cool opportunity, your F*** U Fund allows you to do just that.

As a rule of thumb, the account should have enough money to cover three to six months of fixed expenses. If you are a freelancer and never know when your next paycheck will land, you might prefer to aim for a minimum of six months' average income saved up. If, on the other hand, you have a stable, well-paying job and minimal fixed costs, three months' worth of salary stored away might be more than enough.

No matter what your starting point is, it can feel overwhelming to have such ambitious savings goals—especially if you are starting from scratch. But you can build this up gradually by transferring a small amount every month (or whenever you can). The F*** U Fund comes in handy in many different situations, but essentially it allows you to make financially independent choices, sleep well at night, not be a slave to your employer, and live life on your own terms.

# DEAL WITH DEBT

At some point in our lives most of us will need to take out a loan of some sort, and thereby we will take on some debt. Debt is an amount of money borrowed from someone on the condition that the person borrowing it will pay it back within a certain timeframe. Usually this will be paid back with interest, which is the amount of money a lender receives for lending out money—essentially, the fee for borrowing money.

## DEBT, IS IT ALL BAD... ?

Even though debt sounds like bad news, it doesn't have to be, because a degree of debt is sometimes needed in order to achieve something that benefits Future You. For example, a mortgage that will enable you to purchase a house will not only give you a roof over your head, it will also be a financial asset, which is likely to grow in value over time.

As a rule of thumb, debt used to create value for Future You is good debt. Bad debt, on the other hand, tends to have a high interest rate and does not positively contribute to your future. Credit card debt is typically considered bad debt, especially if it's used to increase your spending unnecessarily. Most credit card debt comes with high interest rates, which is expensive in the long run.

So, what do you do if you already have debt with a high interest rate, or if you need to take on such debt? Well, if the interest rate on any of these debts is higher than 7–10%, consider paying it off before investing and before contributing too much toward your F*** U Fund. This is because it is unlikely that the return from your investments will be higher than that, so as a result, the interest you pay for having a loan will exceed the amount you will get in return from your investments.

# HOW TO PAY OFF DEBT

With rising interest rates, it's in most people's interest to pay down as much personal debt as possible. There are many approaches to tackle this and in the following pages we'll go through two of the most popular ones: the snowball method and the avalanche method.

### The snowball method

This method is all about paying off debt by working up from the smallest balance to the largest. It is great for those who need the visual motivation of watching smaller loans quickly disappear to stay disciplined. While you are doing this, you continue to make minimum debt contributions on all your debts, then use any additional cash that you might have to pay off the smallest loan first.

Take a good look at everything you owe and rank the debts in size order (this is simply the amount that is owed, you are not looking at the interest rates here), with the lowest at the top of your list. This is where you are going to begin. Once that smaller debt is paid off, you move on to the next one, adding the amount you were paying each month on the previous debt, which you no longer need to pay, onto the existing regular payments of the next debt. In other words, each payment snowballs and gets bigger with every debt you pay off.

### Pro

Hopefully you will be able to pay off many smaller loans quickly, which can be extremely motivating and can help you stay on track with your goals.

### Con

This method doesn't focus on the interest rates of your loan, which essentially cost you money, and therefore you are likely to end up paying more in the long term, particularly if you have debts with high interest rates.

# THE SNOWBALL METHOD

**Starts from the top**

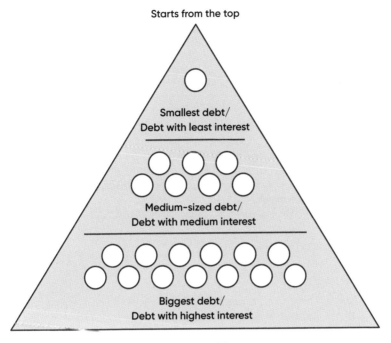

Smallest debt/
Debt with least interest

Medium-sized debt/
Debt with medium interest

Biggest debt/
Debt with highest interest

# THE AVALANCHE METHOD

**Starts from the bottom**

### The avalanche method

With this method, you start by paying off debt with the highest interest rate first. Again, you continue to make the minimum debt contributions required on all your other debts at the same time, and you use any additional cash that you might have available to pay off the loan with the highest interest rate.

Only when this is paid off in its entirety do you move on to the next debt and do the same thing.

### Pro

This is the financially smart thing to do, because the higher the interest rate, the more expensive the loan. Therefore, you save the most in the long term by using this method.

### Con

If the debt with the highest interest rate also has the highest balance, it will take longer to pay it down and you won't get the same satisfaction of simplifying your debts by quickly getting all the smaller loans out of the way.

*Example:*
Let's say you have three loans:

1. A credit card debt with a balance of $20,000, an 18% interest rate and a monthly payment of $400.
2. A car loan with a balance of $36,000, a 15% interest rate and a monthly payment of $150.
3. A student loan with a balance of $10,000, a 7% interest rate and a monthly payment of $300.

Using the avalanche method, you would pay off the credit card debt first because of its high interest rate of 18% (while continuing to also cover the minimum regular payment of $150 to the car loan and $300 to the student loan). Once the entire credit card debt was paid off, you would spend the $400 you used to pay for the credit card toward the car loan, so that you now pay the minimum rate of $150 plus an additional $400, which means you are now paying $550 a month on that.

Using the snowball method, you would first pay off the student loan because it has the lowest balance. Once this was paid off you would move on to the credit card debt, then finish with the car loan.

There is no right or wrong answer here, so pick the method that feels most motivating and effective for you and your situation. The important thing is just that you have a plan and that you are tackling your debt.

# Is Social Security enough?

Retirement can mean different things for different people. It could mean quitting work entirely and travelling the world. Or it might mean transitioning into a part-time position while also pursuing something you love. If you are at the beginning of your career, you are probably not thinking about retirement, or what type of lifestyle you might want when you get to that point. But even though it's not right around the corner, you should still start preparing for it. Preparation is power: The earlier you start saving for retirement, the more freedom you'll have when the time arrives.

In certain countries, the government provides a pension to its citizens, such as Social Security, that is funded by taxed income. However, while helpful, this amount of money is often not enough to maintain the living standard that you probably had when you were working full-time. One way to ensure that you don't have to start scrimping and saving in your older age is to open a retirement account and start contributing to it regularly as soon as you can. Make sure your money is invested consistently in stocks, bonds, investment funds, or something else. Remember, your money should be working for you while you are working.

By investing, you are giving the money in your retirement account the opportunity to grow over time. There are, of course, some risks attached to investing, but historically the stock market has outpaced the rate of inflation in the long run, which means that you would have been better off investing your money, rather than keeping it all in your savings account.

As mentioned earlier, some countries offer some sort of retirement contribution to tax-paying workers, and if you are an employee, as opposed to being self-employed, some companies offer 401k plans as a part of their employment package. If that is not the case for you, you can always set up your own, by contacting a company that offers this service. Some retirement accounts offer tax advantages, but be warned that they can also have some potential drawbacks. For example, you could be charged a substantial amount of additional tax if you withdraw money from a retirement account early.

Basically, these accounts are designed to encourage you to set money aside for retirement and discourage you from being tempted to use the money you have saved before you retire.

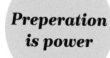

*Preperation is power*

# How much do you need to save for your retirement?

Do your own research or work with a professional, but however you do it, get started as early as possible on an investment plan that takes both your personal goals and an ideal retirement plan into consideration. A key part of retirement planning is to answer the question: "How much do I need to save for retirement?" The answer varies by individual, and it depends largely on your income now, at what age you want to retire, and what lifestyle you would like when you retire. Retirement planning is difficult because no one knows how many years they might need to fund. That's the case for all of us. However, as a rough guideline, most experts say your annual retirement income should be about 80% of your final pre-retirement salary. But, of course, this will depend on how you plan to spend your retirement, and you should also factor in any unforeseen events, such as getting sick and needing to pay for care, or needing to provide care for a loved one.

So, the first step is to envision what your retirement looks like. Will you be working part-time? Will you quit working entirely? Do you want to travel the world? Spend more time with your family and friends? All these scenarios have different budgets and therefore require different levels of funding.

The second thing to consider is your time horizon. In the EU Member States, the average retirement age for both men and women is 65 years old. Think about at what age you would like to stop working. If you want to quit in your fifties, you'll naturally need a bigger retirement pot as you will potentially have more years of retirement to finance.

Once you have established the size of your required retirement savings, you can start to see if your current contributions are enough or if you need to course-correct.

Starting a retirement account early and adding to it often can give Future You more options and flexibility. It's never too soon to begin, and here are your options:

# EARLY STAGES OF YOUR CAREER

You might not be earning a lot of money if you're at the beginning of your career, but you do have one advantage: time. When you're in your twenties or thirties, you can build your retirement savings slowly, which makes the process much more pleasant and exciting. Why? Two words: compound interest.

Compound interest (which we'll tell you more about on page 105) is a term used to describe how savings can grow exponentially. Compound interest basically means you gain interest on top of previous interest earned. This is why starting early is important, as your retirement account will have more time to compound, and even small savings can add up to large sums over time. Much like a snowball effect, you'll gain the most at the very end.

# MID-CAREER

The first step is to figure out if you have already contributed to your retirement in previous jobs through their company plans. If that's the case, it can be worth putting all those different savings into one combined retirement account and starting to add to this on a regular basis.

The second step is to do some research on the different retirement options available to you right now. Does your employer offer a 401k plan? Maybe it's time for that salary negotiation talk and to ask your employer to increase their contributions?

# CLOSE TO RETIREMENT

If you are close to when you would like to retire, you can still benefit from compound interest. However, you don't have the same time horizon, nor, therefore, the same potential to accrue money. But there are still options, so you shouldn't turn a blind eye to your retirement. Instead, brush off your retirement plans and examine how much of any savings that you may have would be worthwhile investing.

**EDITH**

# "It's never too late to get started."

At 75 years old, Edith is the co-founder of an investment club that includes 35 retired women members. The investment club is about finances and female empowerment, and for Edith, age has never been an obstacle. Here she shares her story to remind and persuade others that it's never too late to start investing.

**35 women and $1 million**: I was 60 years old when I first got into investing. I had always been interested in the topic, but I had never actually seen any women doing it, so I thought it wasn't for me. However, in 2007 I convinced some of my friends to found an investment club. We each brought $25,000, which gave us just under $1 million collectively to invest. It was a lot of money to handle, so in the beginning we got help from a financial advisor. It went well at first, but then the financial crisis hit in 2008. Our investments dropped by 80%, but we agreed to stay in the market. Take it or leave it became our motto!

**The investment that keeps on giving**: The investment club is not just about making money, it's about the social aspect as well. Our investments have more than recovered now, and we use some of the profits we make for shared experiences. Every year we arrange at least two trips, so we have travelled the world and enjoyed weekend trips away together. We also hold five meetings a year in which we catch up and discuss our collective finances. Everyone makes a big effort to be actively involved and we have a waiting list of women wanting to join us.

The investment club is all about empowering women. We are all doing well financially but, more importantly, we're fully in control and we do everything ourselves (the financial advisor is long gone!). None of us have ever felt that age was an obstacle, and neither should you. It's never too late to start investing.

**Life is now!** We have a few financial goals that we are collectively working toward in the investment club. Privately, I have achieved my goals. My husband and I have invested our savings and pension, which has given us the freedom to live our best life. I work without a salary because I love my job, and I have the financial freedom to do it. Thanks to our investments, we have everything we want and dream about. Life is happening now, and it needs to be lived!

# Money and relationships

Finding love (or even like) isn't easy, and finding a partner is not just about having a strong connection and making each other laugh, it's also about having the same dreams for the future and agreeing on the ways to get there. Does that sound difficult? It definitely is—and money plays a big part in this.

No matter how much you love your significant other, trying to merge your lives can be a bumpy (but still beautiful!) ride. After all, you have both had different life experiences up until the moment you met, and the way you perceived and internalized those experiences was probably very different. That's why a couple can have two *very* different views on money, which can lead to disagreements. A 2019 study reported that regardless of the happiness level within the relationship, money is a topic that couples consistently disagree about and is the number one issue they fight about—and unsurprisingly it is also a leading cause of divorce.

When talking about money and relationships, it's interesting to look at some general trends and dynamics. Around the world, women in heterosexual relationships tend to take the back seat when it comes to big financial decisions. According to UBS, only 20% of such couples participate equally in financial decisions, with the majority of women leaving long-term financial decisions to their male partner. Interestingly, younger women (aged 20–34) are most likely to defer to their significant others on financial matters. That's not good. We can't just let our partners handle our finances, even if the relationship is going well. Why? Well, assuming you are married, take a minute to consider what happens in case of divorce.

Do you know which accounts are in your joint names? Who gets the house if you split up? What happens with your shared loans? Are there any assets other than the bank or investment accounts that you might be entitled to, in case one of you wants to call it quits? The fact is, 80% of women die single and 74% of women discover negative financial surprises after a divorce or death of their spouse. Not surprisingly, a survey from UBS found that 76% of widows or divorcees wish they had been more involved in long-term financial decisions while they were married, rather than having to navigate them as they were coping with such significant life changes.

Playing an active part in your shared finances is key in securing your future. This also goes for doing unpaid domestic labor and taking time off work to care for children or sick family members. These tasks often fall on women, and they have significant negative financial implications. Therefore, you *need* to make a conscious choice about how you split this burden between yourself and your partner. It might be an uncomfortable conversation, but it definitely won't be as uncomfortable as being financially inferior for the rest of your life.

This is all relevant to heterosexual relationships, but how do women in same-sex relationships manage their finances? While research on the area is scarce, some patterns are clear. According to Robert-Jay Green, who has studied LGBT relationships since 1975, same-sex couples tend to be much more egalitarian in their relationships in many areas including decision-making, finances, housework and childcare. Green concludes: "Basically every dimension we looked at, same-sex couples are dramatically more equal in the way they function together as a couple compared to heterosexual couples."

But if women in same-sex relationships are both engaged in financial decisions, why do women in heterosexual relationships hold back? We don't have the answer to this, but in the following pages we'll give you some tools to move yourself from the back seat to the driver's seat of your financial decisions.

# SILENCE IS SILVER, BUT TALKING IS GOLDEN

Whether you are planning on moving in together, buying a house, getting married, or getting divorced, most stages of a relationship involve mixing finances to some degree. The best way to avoid negative financial surprises and money-related fights is by having open and honest communication from the start. Even though talking about money with your partner is not exactly romantic, it is necessary for any serious relationship.

*One in three of those who argue with their spouse about money confess they have hidden purchases from them.*

It can be good to have these talks at least quarterly, or maybe monthly if that works better for you. Pencil in an evening for this discussion and try to use the time to get on track in terms of your financial situation, your joint budgets, and your shared money goals. This is not only empowering for you, but the good news is that managing your money together is key to a financially happy relationship—a survey found that 78% of couples who talk about money every week said they are happy, while only 50% of couples who talk about money very infrequently said the same thing.

# WHAT'S MINE IS YOURS—OR WHAT?

Some couples think the best way to avoid money arguments is to keep separate bank accounts. Each person's paycheck goes into their own account and bills are paid separately. This may sound like a reasonable plan, but the process often builds resentment over time. It also divides spending power, eliminating much of the financial value of marriage, as well as the ability to plan for long-term goals such as buying a home or securing retirement. Bill-splitting also avoids discussions about how financial burdens will be handled if one person loses a job or changes career. Couples owe it to themselves to have a conversation about such contingencies well before any of them arise.

# POWER PLAYS

In most couples, one person makes more money than the other. But whether the difference is $50 or $50,000 a year, the problem of power plays easily arises. This is especially seen in these four scenarios:

1. One partner has a paid job and the other doesn't.
2. Both partners would like to be working but one is unemployed.
3. One spouse earns considerably more than the other.
4. One partner comes from a family that has money and the other doesn't.

When one or more of these situations is present, the money earner (or the one who makes or has the most money) often wants to dictate the couple's spending priorities. Although there may be some rationale behind this idea, it is still important that both partners work together as a team. Keep in mind that while a joint account offers greater transparency and access to the shared funds, it is not in itself a solution to an unbalanced power/money dynamic in the relationship.

Remember, you're on the same team and you should have an equal say in both your relationship and in your money management, too.

# SET EXPECTATIONS TOGETHER

Personality can play a big role in discussions and habits about money. While some people are natural savers, others are big spenders and take pleasure in shopping.

Identifying your and your partner's money personalities is important, as this will allow you to address and adapt each of your money habits to something that is mutually agreeable. This is especially relevant when planning for the future and discussing money expectations, because unmet expectations can cause a lot of conflict and resentment later on.

When having these discussions, avoid unrealistic expectations; there's no rule stating that married couples have to buy a home, start a family, or go on a trip to Paris during their first year of marriage. If those things aren't feasible for you right now, stop worrying. Get your money in order *now* so that *later* you can make your dreams a reality.

**Couples in healthy marriages are twice as likely to discuss money dreams together.**

# Summing up...

In this chapter we have covered all the fundamental elements of your personal finances. The idea is to equip you with a useful overview of the things we recommend you consider before you start your investing journey—which is what we will discuss in the subsequent chapters.

But before we begin, let's summarize the four tasks we recommend you do before you make your first investment, to give yourself the best—and most responsible—start possible.

**1**

### Create a sustainable budget

Go through your bank statements from the last six to twelve months to get a sense of what you have coming in, and where your money is going. Remember, this is not an exercise to make you feel bad about your spending, but rather to make sure you have an accurate overview of your finances.

Once you have done this, create a budget and do your best to be realistic, so it's easy to stick to. We like the 50/30/20 rule; to recap, that means 50% of your take-home pay should go toward expenses like rent and transport; 30% goes toward fun, because the budget needs to be sustainable; and 20% goes toward the Future You—this includes insurance, investing, and saving.

**2**

### First pay off any high-interest debt you have

We're talking about credit cards or double-digit-interest-rate loans here. It is unlikely that you will be able to get a double-digit return in the stock market, so you would actually do better to pay off your loan first.

### Create a F*** U Fund for emergencies or opportunities

You need to make sure you have enough money saved in case of emergencies, or in case an exciting opportunity arises that you want to pursue. The exact amount you need will vary from person to person, and will among other things depend on your job security. However, we normally recommend having three to six months' worth of expenses held in a high-yield savings account, so you've got it when you need it.

### Think about your pension savings!

Make sure you are on track with your pension fund or retirement savings. Ideally, 20% of your income should go toward Future You, which includes your pension savings (as well as any contribution toward your F*** U Fund and investment portfolio). If you can't make that happen right away, that's ok. Starting slow and building up over time is normal and completely fine. Try saving 1% if that's all you can manage, or perhaps pay in 5% now, then increase it in the future when you get a raise. The key point here is making saving a habit and prioritizing Future You every month.

Once you have considered and made a plan for these four tasks, you are ready to dig into investing. Although the prospect of investing your hard-earned savings might seem overwhelming and frightening at first, we guarantee it's not difficult—actually, most people find it both fun and extremely rewarding once they get the hang of it.

Let's get started!

# NEXT...

# INVEST

# Kickstarting your investment journey

Imagine a world where women had more money; to invest in companies we believe in, to influence political decision-making, and to make independent decisions. Sounds pretty great, right?

So let's break the stereotypes and change the narrative of what an investor looks like. And while we're at it, let's inspire other women to do the same. When more women begin investing, we can change the future. Not just our own, but also our collective future. This is possible because investing is like voting with your money. Want to support diverse leadership, sustainable production, or dignified working conditions? Then invest in companies who care. We all have a role to play when it comes to defining the future; it's time we start performing It.

Getting where you want to go in life takes time and money. It's never too early or late to start growing the finances you need to achieve your goals. If you want to pursue financial freedom, you will need to move beyond just boosting savings. In this section we're going to take you through the basics of investing and help you to make that first investment.

Let's change the future. Together. Starting today.

# Did you know?

**Stock trading has existed for more than 400 years—and women joined before they even got the right to vote.**

The first stock exchange was established in Antwerp, Belgium, in 1531, but the first stock was traded in 1611 in Amsterdam, in the Netherlands. However, women were shut out of investing because it was commonly assumed that a male family member would handle a woman's financial decisions. Even though there is evidence for early female participation in the stock market, it wasn't until the 1880s that the first female stockbrokers started to emerge in the US and the UK.

These trailblazing women made their way into the world of investing long before they had the right to vote or own property. They paved the way for future generations, pushing the boundaries of gender roles well before legislation caught up. A lot has happened since then, but the work is far from done. As a private investor, you play an important role. Are you ready to own it?

# What is investing?

The term "investing" covers a lot of different things. In fact, anything you buy with the intention of selling at a higher price could be viewed as an investment, also known as an "asset." This could be anything from vintage wine or cars, to racehorses, designer handbags and artworks. The list is endless. In this book, though, we will zoom in on stocks, investment funds and ETFs. Why these in particular? Well, there are three main reasons:

1. You can get started with just a small amount of money (often as little as $100).
2. They're quick and easy to trade (when the markets are open, a deal often goes through within seconds, which is very different than, say, the process of buying a house).
3. Stocks and funds can yield good returns in the long run. (In fact, the historical average stock market return is 7-10% per year, although this is an average, so some years are much better, while others yield negative returns. Therefore, a 10% return is never guaranteed.)

Before we explore these three assets, we want to provide you with a basic introduction to a few popular asset classes that you have probably come across. Though far from exhaustive, the list below should give you an elementary understanding of each of them. For various reasons, we don't believe they are ideal for first-time investors (at least we highly discourage you from putting all your eggs in one of these investment baskets when you are getting started). That said, though, it's great to diversify your portfolio and it's always useful to understand the underlying mechanics of other investment vehicles, so you can make informed decisions for yourself.

# BONDS

### WHAT ARE THEY?
In simple terms, a bond is a loan from an investor to a borrower, which could be either a company or government. The loan will usually have a fixed time horizon (see page 104), which could be anywhere from a couple of days to 50 years. The borrower uses the loan to finance its operations, and in return the investor receives a small interest on the money loaned.

### WHAT IS THE MAIN BENEFIT?
As their returns are set out from inception and therefore not subject to the whims of investor sentiment, bonds are generally seen as a more stable, low-risk, and steady investment class.

### WHAT IS THE DOWNSIDE?
Risk and reward always go hand in hand. Since the risk associated with investing in bonds is considered to be minimal, the returns you can expect from bonds are also comparatively small.

### WHO IS IT IDEAL FOR?
If you are edging closer to retirement, beginning to withdraw your investments, or have a very low-risk appetite, bonds are a great option because they offer a more predictable return and are not subject to price fluctuations in the way that stocks are.

# CRYPTOCURRENCIES

## WHAT ARE THEY?

Cryptocurrencies—often abbreviated as crypto—are digital or virtual currencies that don't exist in any physical form but live only on a computer network. Many cryptocurrencies use a decentralized blockchain technology to secure funds from one user to the other.

One of the most defining characteristics of cryptocurrencies is that they are usually not issued or governed by a central entity, like a bank, but controlled by the users on the network, and while there are various control and governance mechanisms, they vary greatly between the different cryptocurrencies. The most well-known cryptocurrency is Bitcoin, which today has achieved wider acceptance as a form of payment.

## WHAT IS THE MAIN BENEFIT?

Since they are not controlled by any country or bank, cryptos can be an alternative option when, for example, a country's national currency is subject to very high or even hyperinflation (inflation above 50% during a given month), or the government restricts access to bank accounts. From a pure investment angle, cryptocurrencies have seen very sharp returns in the past. And as many cryptocurrencies are closely linked to technology trends like the metaverse, this could potentially result in future profits.

## WHAT IS THE DOWNSIDE?

With the potential of great returns follows tremendous risk; the biggest being that cryptocurrencies are not regulated. That means that no government is controlling what or how they are being used. There have been countless cases of individual cryptocurrencies that entirely lost their value and became virtually worthless overnight, either due to extremely volatile market dynamics, hackers, or simply because they were a scam. Anything remotely similar is extremely (!) unlikely to happen in the stock market.

## WHO IS IT IDEAL FOR?

Ideally you are a technophile and curious to understand the minute details of the technology itself. You also have to be very risk-tolerant and in some cases willing to lose your invested sum. If this is you, allocating a small portion of your portfolio to some more recognized and established cryptocurrencies (such as Ethereum and Bitcoin) to speculate on high returns might be worth considering.

# ART AND COLLECTABLE ITEMS

## WHAT ARE THEY?

Art typically refers to paintings, sculptures, photographs, etc., which people have been buying and selling for centuries. But there are many more collectable items you can invest in, too, such as vintage wine, classic cars, whiskey, antique watches, digital art such as NFTs (Non-Fungible Tokens), or even toys. Common among them all is that their value—and hence the price—is very hard to assess for an outsider, as it is often highly subjective.

## WHAT IS THE MAIN BENEFIT?

One undoubtedly large benefit of investing in, let's say a painting, is that you can hang it up and actually see your investment. If you know what you are doing you can yield high returns from the right bottle of wine or a limited-edition Rolex.

## WHAT IS THE DOWNSIDE?

The biggest downside is that the future price is dependent on taste, and as an average investor it is very difficult to know the value of your investment at any given time. Also, as opposed to stocks that can always be sold on an exchange within minutes, selling a real item requires more effort and, most importantly, you need to find that one, right buyer who is willing to pay the price that you think (and hope) it's worth.

## WHO IS IT IDEAL FOR?

If you are an art connoisseur or an expert in a particular niche and you enjoy keeping up with the latest trends—whether for old musical instruments, champagne, or collectable comic books—then investing in some rare and precious items can be very lucrative, and even a very enjoyable hobby.

# COMMODITIES

## WHAT ARE THEY?

Commodities are basic goods that can be transformed into other goods and services. The tradition of commodity trading dates back centuries to a time before stocks and bonds ever exchanged hands. From rare spices and silk fabrics in the very early days to the digital exchanges where commodities currently trade, commodities remain very popular investments. Today, the most commonly traded commodities are gold, oil, and base metals. You can either invest directly in the physical commodity, by buying an actual gold bar or a so-called "certificate" that replicates the gold price, or indirectly, for example, by investing in shares of commodity companies or investment funds (more on this later) focusing on a particular commodity.

## WHAT IS THE MAIN BENEFIT?

Demand for commodities tends to be particularly great during periods of high inflation, as the inflation also causes the prices of the commodity to increase. Therefore, a major benefit of investing in commodities is that they offer great diversification and serve as protection against the value of your money depreciating because of inflation. Gold, in particular, is recognized for its ability to hedge against a market downturn.

## WHAT IS THE DOWNSIDE?

Commodities don't come without risk and are typically much more volatile than other kinds of investments, especially funds that track a single commodity or a specific sector of the economy. As with any investment, it's necessary to understand the market fundamentals of the commodity you want to trade—for example, the fact that oil prices often fluctuate in response to changes in the political climate in the Middle East.

 # PROPERTY

## WHAT IS IT?

You invest in real estate, which is either your own home that you live in, or an apartment you rent out. If you are not in a position to buy a full property yourself but still want exposure to the housing market, then an option is to buy shares in REITs (Real Estate Investment Trusts). These are companies that own and often operate a collection of properties, where any profits from rent or increases in value are shared among the shareholders.

## WHAT IS THE MAIN BENEFIT?

This is one of few investments where it is advantageous to take out a loan in order to spend greater sums than you could otherwise afford to. Historically, real estate (at least in urban areas) has increased in value, which means it's been a great way to earn high returns. If you live in your property, you can also count as another benefit the interest you pay on your mortgage is lower than the rent you would otherwise have to pay.

## WHAT IS THE DOWNSIDE?

In most cases you have to put down a sizable down payment, and the higher that number, the better the terms of the mortgage will be. Also, as you become the owner of a physical property, there are many responsibilities, such as repairs, maintenance and tax, which need to be considered. If you invest in property to rent it out and earn additional income, there is always the risk of poor tenants who don't pay rent on time or cause damage, which ultimately you are responsible for. Finally, when you own a large physical asset it cannot easily be moved around, so if for some reason the area where your property is located decreases in value, your investment will also be affected.

## WHO IS IT IDEAL FOR?

Investing in property is ideal for anyone who can afford to do so. The housing market is inherently different from city to city and country to country, so while it might be possible for a low-income individual to buy a nice house in a very rural area, it might be impossible for someone even with a high income to buy a two-bedroom flat in Manhattan, London, or other metropolitan areas.

# Introduction to stocks and investment funds

Being faced with the jargon and the options available can feel overwhelming. But fear not, we are here to explain to you what these are and give you the know-how to navigate the investment jungle with total confidence. Remember, women are better investors, and this is your moment to change the way your finances are working for you.

Knowledge is power, so let's start with the basics.

## Did you know?

Studies show that women achieve better returns than men when investing because they trade less frequently, spend more time on research before they buy, and take on more appropriate levels of risk.

# STOCKS

Before you begin investing, you need a basic understanding of the world you are about to enter. The first step? Demystifying the stock market.

Put simply, in many ways the stock market works rather like a farmers' market, where buyers and sellers meet to trade. Even though these stocks are traded virtually, the physical market is a helpful way of visualizing just how the system works. Like products at a farmers' market, stocks are priced according to supply and demand; if demand for a specific stock increases, the price will go up.

You cannot trade directly on the stock exchange, which is why you need to use an online trading platform; this could be either your bank or an external platform, and we will go over this later on page 163. However, regardless of the platform you choose to use, the price of the stock will be the same.

## HOW THE STOCK MARKET WORKS

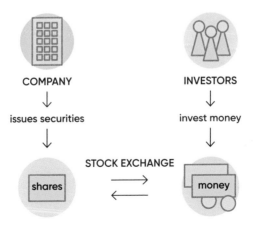

COMPANY
↓
issues securities
↓

INVESTORS
↓
invest money
↓

STOCK EXCHANGE

shares ⟶  money
      ⟵

# The rise and fall of the stock market

When investing in stocks, it is important to be aware that their value can both rise and fall. According to the S&P 500 (a stock market index that tracks 500 of the US's largest companies) the average return for the stock market has historically increased by around 10% per year. This number is often used as a benchmark to measure the average performance of the stock market, but to reiterate, this number is an *average*, so it therefore includes years in which the returns are much better and/or much worse. However, the overall trend is clear—over time, returns in the market have gone up in about 70% of the years during which the stock market has existed.

## STOCK VALUE OF THE S&P 500 INDEX SINCE 1975

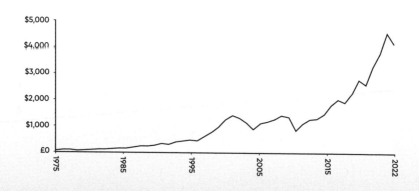

# WHAT ARE STOCKS?

Stocks represent ownership. When you are buying stocks in a specific company, you're effectively purchasing an ownership share in it. Does that mean you get to sit next to Elon Musk at Tesla's next shareholder meeting? No. But in most cases it does mean you get the right to vote at those meetings, if you choose to exercise it. And you should—this is an excellent opportunity to influence the decisions of large companies and get your voice heard in places where women have historically been excluded from participating.

Your rights as an investor also depend on how many shares you own (stocks and shares are the same, but whereas "stock" often describes stocks in general, "share" often refers to the stocks of a specific company). If a company issues 100 shares and you buy one, you own 1% of the company. However, companies often issue millions of shares, so as a private investor you then own only a tiny part of the company. For example, Amazon has more than 500 million shares at the time of writing. If you own 100 Amazon shares, that's equal to 0.0000002% of the company.

So, buying stocks allows ordinary people to invest in some of the most successful companies in the world, albeit in a small way. For the companies themselves, selling stocks is of benefit to them because it is a way to raise money to fund growth, products, and other initiatives for their business.

## WHERE ARE STOCKS STORED?

You've probably seen old movies with chaotic scenes of people screaming at each other across the trading floor, waving pieces of paper in the air and shouting, "Buy, buy, buy! Sell, sell, sell!" That's what the stock market used to look like, but today all trades are electronically registered and everything happens online.

Most countries have a Central Securities Depository, which is an institution that holds financial instruments such as stocks and bonds. This is important to mention because it gives you unique safety; if you forget the password to your trading platform (or if you forget that you even own stocks), you don't lose ownership of your stocks.

## THE TWO MAJOR TYPES OF STOCKS

The economy is divided into cycles; this term refers to the fluctuations of the economy between periods of expansion (growth) and periods of contraction (recession). These cycles impact different companies and industries in different ways, so it's important to keep them in mind when you are considering making an investment.

How stocks react to changes in the overall economy is often determined by what industry they belong to. There are two main types of stocks: cyclical and non-cyclical.

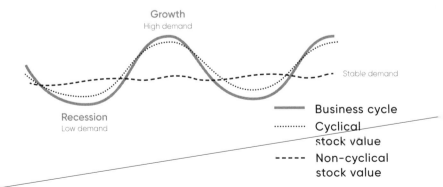

Growth
High demand

Recession
Low demand

Stable demand

—— Business cycle

·········· Cyclical
stock value

----- Non-cyclical
stock value

## Cyclical stocks

Cyclical stocks tend to follow trends in the economy. These companies sell goods and services that consumers buy when the economy is doing well and they have more money to play with, but that they will cut out during economic downturns. This includes luxury goods, restaurants, hotel chains and airlines. More money in the economy means more demand for these products or services, resulting in an increased revenue that will ultimately benefit the shareholders, because cyclical stocks often increase significantly in value during such periods of economic growth. However, these stocks are often hit harder when economic growth slows down and money becomes tighter for consumers. So, because cyclical stocks are so dependent on the overall market, they usually have higher volatility, which also means that they are expected to produce higher returns during periods of economic strength.

**Pros**

Higher returns during periods of economic growth.

**Cons**

Value hit harder during economic downturns.

## Non-cyclical stocks

Companies that fall into the non-cyclical category are fairly stable because they can make money regardless of how the overall economy is doing. This is possible because they produce essential goods or services that people will need and choose to pay for regardless of their financial situation. This includes companies within healthcare, pharmaceuticals, and food production. As a result, these stocks are affected less when the economy slows down and they tend to outperform the market during times of crisis. When the economy is booming, non-cyclical stocks don't experience the same increase in demand as cyclical stocks, and therefore their stock price doesn't increase as much.

### Pros
Relatively stable, outperform the market during economic slowdown.

### Cons
Don't experience high growth during periods of economic prosperity.

### Which should you choose?

So now you know what's on offer, how do you choose between cyclical and non-cyclical stocks when you are putting together your investment portfolio? In short, it all depends on your appetite for risk. If you prefer more predictable, stable returns, non-cyclical stocks might be for you. However, if you're not frightened by higher risk and want a potentially higher return, cyclical stocks might be a better option.

There is no right or wrong answer, it is totally up to you and what makes you feel financially comfortable. You can also mix the two, having a base of non-cyclical stocks, which you buy and hold for many years; then you can add a top layer of cyclical stocks, which you can exchange depending on the overall state of the economy and your changing finances.

| Business | Examples |
|---|---|
| **CYCLICAL** | |
| - Performance follows the trends in the overall economy<br>- Products are non-essential | - Jewellery<br>- Cars<br>- Vacation industries |
| **NON-CYCLICAL** | |
| - Performance is not impacted by trends in the overall economy<br>- Products are essential | - Food<br>- Medication<br>- Electricity |

# GROWTH AND VALUE STOCKS

To make matters more complex, stocks can be divided into two further categories: growth and value stocks. Understanding these divisions will help you put together a well-balanced portfolio and align it with your expected risk and return.

### Growth stocks

A growth stock is any share in a company that's expected to grow faster than the average market. This often includes companies with a very scalable business model, for instance, those in the tech industry where companies don't depend on physical infrastructure. As with all investing, you need to balance risk and return, because while growth stocks provide a great potential for future return, they often have an equally high risk factor. The main risk is that the high growth does not continue in the future, which can cause the stock price to fluctuate significantly. Since the early 2000s, growth stocks have outperformed the overall market; some famous growth stocks include Amazon, Facebook, and Apple.

### Value stocks

Value stocks are defined as companies that are currently traded at a cheaper value than they are actually worth. There can be many reasons why a stock is undervalued, including short-term events like bad publicity for a company or product, or long-term events such as poor conditions in the industry in which the company operates (such as new legislation or increased production prices). Deciding whether a stock is undervalued takes a great amount of research, which new investors are often unable to undertake. However, the term is still important to know, as it can be a valuable tool when choosing investment funds (don't worry, we'll get to that later).

As well as understanding the pros and cons of growth or value stocks, to determine whether you should buy them you also need to consider your time horizon (see page 104) and the amount of risk you can afford.

# STOCKS: DOES SIZE MATTER?

Stocks come in all shapes and sizes. To help you navigate these, they are divided into categories based on their market value. These categories are called "caps," and they include small-cap, mid-cap, and large-cap stocks. Put simply, the bigger the cap, the bigger the company.

Historically, small-cap companies have tended to be riskier investments than large-cap companies. Even though they might have greater growth potential in the long run, they do not have the same resources as larger companies, which makes them more vulnerable to negative events. As a result, the stock price of small-cap companies often fluctuates more than that of larger companies. Despite the higher risk attached to small-cap companies, many investors still find them attractive, as they often have high growth potentials. Looking at large-cap companies, they tend to be less volatile and are more likely to pay out dividends (see page 94), which is seen as a plus by many investors.

Not sure what to choose? We get it. But remember, when it comes to stock picking, there is no one answer, no absolute right or wrong. In the end, it depends on your level of experience, time horizon, and risk profile (more on this on page 101). The joy of investments is that you can choose to do whatever fits in with your life and financial situation at the time of buying, and have the freedom to change this up as your finances change, take higher or lower risks, or cash in if you need to. You can choose investments for the short term, or think ahead for the long term to build a better pension.

# The joy of investment is that you can choose to do whatever fits in with your life and financial situation.

# Using a P/E value to make your investment decisions

If you need something a bit more tangible, one of the most popular metrics that investors use to decide whether a company's stock price is under- or overvalued is price to earnings value, or P/E. This metric can be used to evaluate the price of stock from one company compared to other companies in the same industry. The ratio is calculated by dividing the price per share by the company's earnings per share. But this figure will often be stated on your trading platform, so you don't have to actually do the maths yourself.

The benefit of the ratio is that it helps you assess the price of the stock, as compared to the company's earnings. If a company has a P/E of, let's say, 25, that means its stocks are traded at 25 times its earnings. The high multiple indicates that investors expect higher growth in the company, compared to the overall market. In short, the P/E shows what the market is willing to pay today for a stock, based on the company's past or future earnings.

A high P/E could mean that a stock's price is expensive relative to how much the company is actually earning, and therefore potentially overvalued. On the other hand, a low

P/E might indicate that the stock price is cheap relative to the current earnings of the company. Investors not only use the P/E ratio to determine a stock's market value but also to assess the future earnings potential. For example, if earnings are expected to rise, investors might expect the company to increase its dividend payments. As a result, higher earnings and a rise in dividends typically lead to a higher stock price.

So, can you use the P/E to compare stocks from different industries against each other, too? The simple answer is no. Companies that grow faster than average, such as technology firms, typically have a higher P/E, and a higher P/E ratio shows that investors are willing to pay a higher share price today, because of growth expectations in the future. The average P/E ratio for the S&P 500 has historically ranged from 13 to 15.

A high P/E does not always mean that a company is overvalued, though, and a low P/E does not always mean that a company is undervalued. Therefore the P/E should not be the only thing you consider, but it can be a good indication of how attractive the stock is.

As a word of caution, if you are new to investing, you might want to begin with the safer, less-volatile options before moving into riskier investments as your confidence builds. Regardless of what you choose, investing is an essential part of building your future and reaching your goals. It's not about being rich when you start out or having a degree in finance. Anyone can learn to invest their money—if they start by investing their time. With each woman who begins investing, we are one step closer to closing the financial gender gap.

# "Investing at an early age empowered me."

At the age of 22, Emma Kvist Nielsen was convinced about the importance of investing. Starting young, with very limited funds, has empowered her in more ways than she could have imagined. She is now determined to spread the word and is trying to encourage other young women to start investing.

**How it started:** I was having coffee with one of my girlfriends, who is a journalist. She was working on a big project about women and investing, which she talked about passionately. After months of research, she bought her first stocks. I had been curious about the stock market for some time, as many of my male friends often discuss stocks and crypto. To me, it seemed like a masculine world that I couldn't be part of, but after my girlfriend expressed the importance of women investing I felt so inspired that I went home and followed suit.

**Chasing dreams:** When I started my investment journey, I thought it was just about achieving my financial goals. But it quickly became something even greater, because what I discovered was that investing is about more than money. I was only 22, with limited financial means, and I had no idea how much it would change my future. It made me feel empowered and in control of so many areas of my life. Recently, my focus has shifted toward sustainability and investing in projects I feel passionately about.

**The difficult conversation:** I get energized when having conversations about finances, but I've realized that some of my friends feel uncomfortable discussing money matters. I still try to push the conversation, because it's so important to be transparent and inspire each other to achieve more in a safe space. That way, we can work toward closing the financial gender gap.

# Anyone can learn to invest their money— if they start by investing their time.

# Summing up

## SMALL-CAP STOCKS

**Pros**
- They often have more growth potential.
- Tend to offer greater returns over the long term.

**Cons**
- More volatile than large-cap companies.
- They have a higher risk compared to large-cap companies.

## LARGE-CAP STOCKS

**Pros**
- Typically a safer investment with less volatility.
- More likely to pay dividends.
- They tend to offer more stable returns in the long run.

**Cons**
- Due to their size, they might adapt more slowly to new trends and events.
- They tend to offer less immediate growth potential.

# Did you know?

**There are more CEOs among the UK's 350 largest companies (FTSE 350) that are named Peter than there are women CEOs in total.**

In the US, CEOs with the name John outnumber women CEOs and in Australia the figure is for both Peter and John! Two-thirds of companies do not have any women in their executive committee. Does that make you angry? Well, it should. But systematically excluding women from leadership positions is not just bad behavior, it is also bad business. This has statistical backing, because companies that have executive committees made up of more than one-third women have net profit margins that are 10 times greater than companies with no women. Maybe that's something to consider when you're researching your next investment?

## MALE AND FEMALE CEOS IN THE FTSE 350

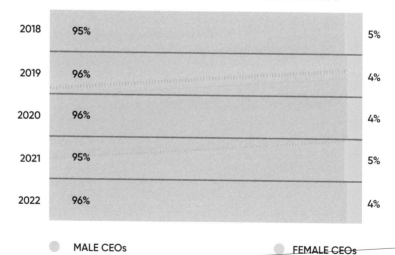

| | | |
|---|---|---|
| 2018 | 95% | 5% |
| 2019 | 96% | 4% |
| 2020 | 96% | 4% |
| 2021 | 95% | 5% |
| 2022 | 96% | 4% |

MALE CEOs          FEMALE CEOs

# How to make money from stocks

So this is the bit you've been waiting for! We all know that the main reason why investors buy stocks is to earn a return, but making money from stocks is not just about being able to buy more things; remember, it's also about financial freedom, independence, and being in charge of your future.

There are two main ways you can make money from stocks:

- **The stock price appreciates—which, simply put, means it goes up.** When this happens, you can sell the stock for a profit, if you like. Over the long term, the average annual stock market return is around 8%. That means if you had invested $1,000 in stocks 30 years ago, that would be worth over $10,000 today. (Another great example of why forward planning and getting control of your finances as early as possible is so important! See page 38.)
- **Some stocks pay dividends.** Dividends are payments made to shareholders out of the company's revenue, and the share price typically decreases by the same amount as the dividend that has been paid out. Not all stocks pay dividends, but many do.

# Deep dive on dividends

A dividend is announced by a company's management and is distributed to shareholders. It's an amount that is paid per share of stock—so if you own 10 stocks in a company and that company pays $2 in dividends, you will receive $20. Often, the stock price decreases by the same amount as the dividends that were paid out. Therefore, dividends are not pure profit but rather an exchange of value from your stocks to cash in your bank account.

It's up to the individual company to decide whether they want to pay out dividends. This decision is made every year at their general assembly, and it's often based on how the company has performed that year. Even though some companies have a long tradition of paying out dividends, there is no guarantee that this repeats in the future, so this should be a consideration when you invest, and not an assumption.

There are mixed opinions about whether dividends are a pro or a con. On one hand, dividends can be an advantage because they provide liquidity (cash) without selling any shares and without paying any fees. At the same time, often stocks fairly quickly increase to the same price that they were before dividends were paid out.

On the other hand, most countries have a dividend tax you need to pay when you receive the money that's been paid out. If the company had not paid out dividends, the money would have stayed in the company. If you want to reinvest the dividends, you therefore have less to reinvest after paying taxes.

## UNDERSTANDING DIVIDENDS

Stocks in Company X cost $300 per stock when the company decides to pay out dividends of $10 per stock. As a result, the stock price drops to $290 per stock.

Sara owns 10 shares in Company X. Before the dividends were paid out, those shares were worth $3,000 (10 stocks x $300). Has she now made or lost money?

The answer is neither. She now owns 10 stocks worth $2,900 and she got dividends worth $100 paid out. Therefore, Sara still has a net worth of $3,000 ($2,900 + $100), which is equal to the value of her stocks before the dividends were paid out.

## Did you know?

Globally, more than 40,000 companies are traded publicly (although this number is increasing as more companies get listed). Despite the large number of publicly traded companies, only a few are run by women. In the UK, only 8% of the largest public companies have a female CEO, while this number is 15% for the largest companies in the US.

# REMEMBER TAX!

Every investment has associated costs. Of all the expenses, taxes can sting the most and take the biggest bite out of your profits.

In many countries, investment income—such as dividends and capital gains—is taxed at a different rate than wage income. The rates differ from country to country, so you need to do some research to find out how much tax you will be charged for your capital gains.

It's important to take these costs (transaction fees and tax) into consideration every time you make a new investment, because in order to actually make a profit, the return has to be bigger than the costs. This is why it's a good idea to avoid investing multiple small amounts. Instead, save up enough money to do one bigger investment at a time.

# MUTUAL FUNDS

When groups of investors join forces and make mutual investments, it's called a mutual fund. In this way, money collected from many investors is used to purchase securities like stocks, bonds, or similar investments. As such, the value of the mutual fund depends on the performance of the securities it buys. So when you buy shares in a mutual fund, it represents investments in many different securities.

When investing in mutual funds, you will always be charged an annual operating fee. This fee is used to cover the administrative costs of the fund, and it usually ranges from 0.01 to 3%. The size of the fee depends on whether the fund is actively or passively managed. This is a service fee to the bank/financial institution who owns the fund and it is automatically subtracted from your investment.

## HOW MUTUAL FUNDS WORK

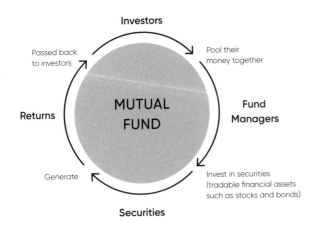

# ACTIVE AND PASSIVE MUTUAL FUNDS

There are two types of mutual funds: active and passive.

**Active mutual fund:** This has employees who analyse the market and pick a combination of investments based on expectations for the market in the future. The goal is to achieve a higher return than the market average. Active funds often have annual fees above 1%.

**Passive mutual fund:** As the name suggests, a passive mutual fund follows the course of a certain index. The goal is to keep the costs low while getting the average market return, rather than beating it. Passive funds often have annual fees below 1%.

So how do you determine if a fund is active or passive? Well, the easiest way is to look at the description of the fund, which often states both its strategy and whether it is actively managed. Another way is to look at the annual fee, as higher fees indicate active management.

# Did you know?

Research suggests that female fund managers tend to deliver better returns. However, only 11% of US fund managers are women, and in the UK there are more fund managers named David than there are female fund managers in total. So, when choosing an active fund, taking a closer look at who the fund manager is might be a good idea.

**Pros of mutual funds:**
- **Diversification:** When investing in a mutual fund, you automatically invest in multiple securities, so mutual funds offer more diversification than individual securities.
- **Professional management**—Mutual funds are managed by professional investors who trade on behalf of the fund.

**Cons of mutual funds:**
- **Low risk, low return:** Mutual funds consist of many different securities, so they fluctuate less than individual stocks. As a result, mutual funds are often said to have a lower risk and thereby also a lower potential return.
- **Fees:** Unlike stocks, mutual funds charge annual fees. These fees vary between funds, and they are charged regardless of how the fund performs.

# What is an index?

An index is used to track the performance of a certain type of stock, a specific sector, or a country's stock market. For example, the NYSE US 100 index tracks the 100 largest companies listed on the New York Stock Exchange.

# ETFs

We can't talk about mutual funds without talking about Exchange-Traded Funds (ETFs). ETFs are a type of passive fund that follows an Index. As with mutual funds, one share of the ETF gives the buyer ownership of all the investments in the fund. For example, if an ETF holds 100 stocks, investors get a stake in all 100 stocks (even though this stake might be small).

As opposed to the actively managed mutual funds, ETFs are passively managed, with the fund holding a set number of stocks based on a specific preset index of investments. ETFs are typically cheaper than mutual funds because the maintenance costs are very low—usually this is around 0.5% of your total investment in the fund, paid annually. However, some ETFs have costs as low as 0.1%, which is significantly below anything you would find in a mutual fund.

## WHAT TO CONSIDER WHEN CHOOSING A MUTUAL FUND/ETF

- **Focus:** Make sure the mutual fund/ETF is invested in something you believe in, whether that's an industry, region or value.
- **Fees:** Even small fees have a big impact on your return over time, therefore you should optimize and go for the cheaper option.
- **Historic performance:** Even though historic performance is no guarantee for the future, it may give an indication of whether the fund is on to something.

# Risk and time horizon

Before you begin investing, you need to consider risk and your time horizon (see page 104). These factors are important because they will help you determine what you should invest in and how much of your money you are comfortable investing.

## RISK

Although investing is a great tool to make money while you sleep, there are no guarantees of success. All investments involve some degree of risk; low-risk investments tend to give smaller and more stable returns, while high-risk investments generally have larger fluctuations and potential for higher returns. Therefore, it's important to consider how risk-averse you are. This will depend on your personality, your financial situation, and your time horizon. Are you afraid of losing money? Then you are not alone. Research consistently shows that women are more risk-averse than men. While this is often highlighted as a negative trait that keeps women from getting started investing, it doesn't have to be. Because this fear is also part of what makes women such great investors once they get involved. Understanding and respecting risk decreases the danger of becoming overconfident and the urge to try to beat the market—both of which are easy ways to lose money. The moral of the story? Embrace your fear—it's your secret super power.

But how do you manage risk? One way is by looking at the split between different asset classes in your portfolio. We give an overview of these on page 152, but here are some key considerations.

- **Choose your investments carefully**—Stocks generally have a higher level of risk than both mutual funds and ETFs (see page 100). This is because ETFs and mutual funds consist of many different investments, and therefore the positive performance of some investments can neutralize the negative performance of others. In this way, you can adjust the risk level of your portfolio by adjusting the split between stocks and funds.
- **Diversify within stocks and funds**—This means investing across continents and industries so that negative events in one country or industry don't impact your entire portfolio. As a rule of thumb, having a diversified portfolio requires you to include at least 10–20 different stocks, which we'll talk more about on page 112.
- **Consider your personal situation**—when assessing your risk profile, some of the most important factors to think about are:
  - ◊ **Age:** It's never too late to begin investing and making money work for you and your future finances, but you might pursue different strategies depending on where you are in life. If you think you will need the money you invest within the next 5–10 years (for example, for retiring or buying a house), you might want to take less risk than if you can afford to wait longer.

*Embrace your fear, it's your secret super power.*

- **Income:** Do you have a fixed income? How much is left after paying your regular expenses? The bigger your buffer, the more risk you can afford.
- **Savings:** How big are your savings? As described on page 44, keeping a F*** U Fund to hand for any unforeseen events is important.

# Did you know?

The number one financial regret among women is not investing enough.

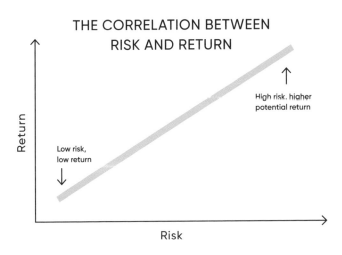

## THE CORRELATION BETWEEN RISK AND RETURN

Return

High risk, higher potential return

Low risk, low return

Risk

# Time horizon

Even though it's tempting to focus on short-term gains, having a long time horizon is key when investing. As a rule of thumb, you can take on more risk the longer your time horizon. Popular opinion holds that you need a time horizon of at least five years, but preferably this should be much longer, because historically the stock market experiences large fluctuations in the short run. Whether these fluctuations are caused by pandemics or political events, they are a normal part of the investment cycle, but despite this volatility, the stock market has always bounced back and increased in value in the long run. Therefore, only invest money you can afford to keep in the market for a longer time period, so you are not forced to sell at a bad time when you suddenly need the money.

*Only invest money you can afford to keep in the market for a longer time period.*

# Compound interest

Compound interest is what makes investing truly life-changing over time... Don't worry, it's not as complicated as it sounds! The simplest explanation of compound interest is that you earn a return on the return you have previously earned. Still not clear? Let's look at an example:

You invest $1,000 in the stock market. Within the first year, your investment increases by 10%, equivalent to $100. The value of your investment is now $1,100 and you keep it for another year without changing anything. The next year, your investment increases by 10% again, and now that is equivalent to $110 because you're also making money off last year's gain ($1,100 total). You now leave this investment without changing anything. After 10 years, the initial investment of $1,000 is now worth $2,593 and after 20 years it has increased to $6,727. The value of your investment will accelerate over time as you earn on both the initial investment and the growing return.

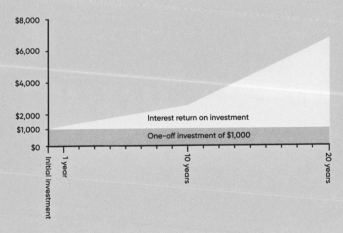

The value of your investment will accelerate over time as you earn on both the initial investment and the growing return.

# What type of investor are you?

Now you've learned the basics of risk and time horizon, you're ready to decide what type of investor you are. So before you hand over your hard-earned cash, here are a few things to ask yourself to make sure you are covering all aspects of your personal finances, from day-to-day expenses to longer-term financial planning.

- **What is your time horizon?** The longer your time horizon, the more risk you can tolerate. A time horizon below five years is often considered to be short, because no one knows what happens in the short run on the stock market.
- **How does your overall financial situation look?** Before investing, you need to be financially stable. If you are unemployed, have high-interest loans or are struggling to pay your fixed expenses, you may want to reconsider if this is the right time for you to start investing.
- **How much money do you want to invest?** If your financial situation allows room for investing, you can get started for as little as $100, as long as the fees on your platform don't make up more than 0.5% of the total investment. Even a small amount of money can grow to a large amount over time.

# 3

# Six golden rules

Now you know the basics, you should be ready to dive in deeper.

But before you take the plunge and make your very first investment, we've outlined six golden rules you might want to keep in mind.

# 01 BUY AND HOLD

When it comes to investing, patience is queen, because even though no one has a crystal ball and can know how the stock market will look tomorrow, next week or next month, we do know that historically its value has always increased in the long term.

For most people the stock market is a scary place precisely because of this unpredictability. But even though the stock market has experienced crises and major fluctuations along the way, it has always bounced back. And it hasn't just bounced back, it has increased toward new heights. For the past 93 years, the stock market has increased in value at an average of 10% per year. As with any average, this includes both better and less well-performing years. Therefore, staying patient and holding your nerve is key to making money in the long term.

# 02 INVEST GRADUALLY

Are you holding back from investing because you're afraid the stock market will tank soon? Then this tip is for you. We all dream of buying when prices are low and then selling when they peak, but the truth is, no one knows if prices today are low or high, because we don't know how the market will develop tomorrow.

Therefore, if you have a sum of money that you'd like to invest, remember that you don't need to invest everything at once. Instead, you can take that money and divide it into smaller portions, which you then invest at different points in time. For example, you could invest some of it today, some in three months, some in six months, and so on.

There's no rule for exactly how long you should wait between each investment or whether you should keep buying the same thing or buy something else. The basic idea is just to invest at different points of the market cycle to make sure you are always present and to avoid buying at the peak. This principle is also known as "dollar cost averaging," which you can read more about on page 157.

## Did you know?

The Federal Reserve (the central bank of the United States) was founded in 1913. Since then, the dollar's value has fallen by 96% while the value of the stock market has increased by 3,138,470%.

# **03** DIVERSIFY YOUR PORTFOLIO

Diversification is key to long-term success on the stock market. When picking individual stocks, we know there are no guarantees as to which will do well, because even though a company might seem solid, unforeseen events could happen (such as a global pandemic!) or the market conditions in that industry could change. Therefore, it is a more sensible idea to spread your risk across multiple different stocks.

A lot of research has been done on this topic, which has revealed that in order to have a diversified portfolio you need to have at least 10–20 different stocks. Also, these stocks should come from different industries and different countries, because then if something happens that affects just one country or one industry, it won't affect your entire portfolio.

If choosing more than 10 stocks sounds a little bit overwhelming, remember you've only just learned about funds. When investing in funds, you indirectly invest in lots of different things. Therefore, an easy way to diversify is to invest in broader funds, which cover the world market or other large indices.

*To have a diversified portfolio you need to have at least 10-20 different stocks.*

# 04 DO YOUR HOMEWORK

Before buying stock you need to do your research. While that doesn't mean you need to become an expert, it does mean you need to understand the basics of what you are investing in. For example, you might invest in a company because you like its business model and believe there will be a future demand for its products or services. It also could be an industry you really believe in—you might want to invest in windmills if you think there will be an increasing demand for green energy in the future.

These are just examples, and the main point of this tip is to advise you to avoid trading-based rumors, hype, or gut feelings.

When talking about what you *need to consider* before buying stocks, let's also talk about what you *do not* need to consider, because a common misperception about investing is that you need to read a ton of financial statements and annual reports when choosing what to invest in. In fact, lots of people seem to believe this so firmly that it prevents them getting started investing in the first place. However, the truth is that for people with no prior understanding of the industry, company, or stock market in general, reading these documents would not make a difference anyway. When you are a long-term investor, it's not about the individual investments you make but rather how they fit the diversification of your overall portfolio.

# 05 DECIDE WHEN TO SELL

You are probably wondering when exactly you should sell an investment. We all want to sell at the perfect time, but the reality is, there is no crystal ball. No one can predict what is going to happen on the stock market, and for the same reason no one knows when is the best time to sell.

If you are investing for the long term, it's important to decide when you are going to sell as soon as you make the investment decision. The key reason for that might sound provocative, but ultimately it's to protect you from yourself. Regardless of your gender, age, or level of experience, you are human, and as humans, when we invest money we worked hard to earn, we get emotional. When that money decreases in value we become fearful, and when it increases in value we become greedy. These emotions are the fastest way to make irrational decisions and lose money on the stock market. Therefore, deciding when to sell at the beginning of your investment can help you keep a clear mind in stressful situations while you are watching the market.

If, on the other hand, you have a shorter time horizon or trade very frequently, there is a tool you can use to avoid feeling the need to monitor your investments very closely. It's called stop-loss and it comes in two variations: stop-loss and trailing stop-loss. You use the first variation, stop-loss, in order to avoid a big loss in case the stop price drops and you need to decide the price that will trigger the stop-loss. As fluctuations are very common in the stock market, it's important that you choose a price point that takes this into account, by allowing the price to drop a small amount without the stop-loss being triggered.

The second variation, trailing stop-loss, works differently. Instead of deciding on a nominal amount, you choose a percentage decrease to trigger it. Let's say that your investment has increased by 30% and you are considering selling to take home the win. You are not sure if the price will continue to increase and you don't want to lose out on any additional upside, so you set a trailing stop-loss. This allows the price to increase and it will only be triggered when the price decreases by the percentage you have set. This way, trailing stop-loss allows you to capture the upside while limiting the risk.

You should be aware that for both variations, someone needs to buy your stocks before the stop-loss is activated and your stocks are sold. This happens automatically, but it might take a while if it's a less-traded stock.

If you have decided on a long-term strategy and you're in it for the long run (as we hope you are), stop-loss tools are less relevant, because if you plan to keep an investment for ten-plus years, it doesn't matter what happens tomorrow. However, if you don't have a long time horizon, or you're someone who sleeps poorly at night worrying about their investments, then maybe it's worth considering, as it automates the sale of your investments and limits any financial damage in case of a big drop in the stock price.

## WHEN ARE GOOD MOMENTS TO SELL?

- When the stock has increased/decreased by a certain amount.
- When that specific stock makes up too much of your portfolio and is making it imbalanced.
- When you think the stock is overrated.
- After a certain time period.

# 06 BE CRITICAL

Our final rule is to always be critical...

Be critical of anyone who tries to convince you to buy a specific stock or fund—especially if those people are also selling the product they want you to buy. This is because you don't want to be influenced by what other people think, the rumors they might spread about a specific company, or the general market development.

This sounds obvious, but it's actually much easier said than done. Someone might give you a tip; it could be a random person on the bus talking about a specific stock, or some cocky person who has been investing professionally for years, but you know better than just taking his or her words for granted and buying whatever they claim is the next cash cow. You know that it's important to do your own research before gambling (yes, if you don't know what you are buying, it constitutes gambling) your hard-earned money.

No one knows what is going to happen in the stock market tomorrow, so, we repeat—stay critical toward advice from everyone. And that even includes your bank advisor, family members, friends, what you read in the news, and so on.

Instead, trust yourself and your gut feeling. You know more than you think!

*Choosing stocks is not about the individual investment; it's about your portfolio as a whole and how well it reflects the average market.*

# "I lost everything on my first investment."

When 41-year-old Anissa started her investment journey, she did the one thing you should never do: she invested all her money in one stock—and lost it all. Instead of giving up, though, Anissa came back strong, and she is now making it a priority to teach her daughter all about finance and investments, and the importance of being financially free. Here are her top tips on bouncing back and sharing the knowledge.

### Get started, but do the research!
My investment journey started when I was on maternity leave with my first child. I had heard a lot about investing through my husband and male colleagues, so I thought it was a great time to get started. Unfortunately, I didn't take the time to do my research, so I did all the wrong things at first. So, what did I do? I invested all my savings in a single stock. Huge mistake! I was extremely unlucky because the most unlikely thing happened. The stock ended up dropping 95%, so I lost all of my money. And not only did I lose my own money, I had also convinced my mother to join my investment with her savings. I didn't have the courage to tell her what happened, so I had to cover her loss. I have actually never told her.

**Rising from the ashes:** It was very hard to accept that I had lost my hard-earned money, but instead of giving up on investing, I was convinced I could do better. I started doing the research I should have done in the first place, and then I tried again. This time, my portfolio contained 12 different stocks with 60% value stocks and 40% growth stocks. It worked, and today I'm proud to call myself a millionaire.

**Teaching my 12-year-old daughter to invest:** Financial education is not on the school curriculum, which I believe is a big mistake. Therefore I'm dedicated to teaching both my son and my daughter about money and finance. I introduced them to the stock market at a very young age, too, so they will have the same advantages in life. They now have their own small stock portfolios with companies they've chosen themselves.

**Closing the financial gender gap:** My daughter is now a very engaged investor, and I hope this financial confidence will give her a future that's full of freedom. Educating our daughters the same way we do with our sons is the key to closing the financial gender gap.

# You've got this—so let's get started!

Getting control of your finances might feel scary, but no one will ever care as much about your money as you will, and no one will do such a thorough job in managing it. So you need to be informed, you need to have a plan and—most importantly—you need to be in the driver's seat of your own economy.

Remember, when you give women the ability to make the most of their money, the world becomes a stronger and better version of itself.

We have now been through all the fundamentals of investing and hopefully you are feeling inspired and excited to start securing your financial future. Opposite is a summary of the major points that we have covered so far—you can use it to double check that your finances are fully optimized and that you are 100% ready to start investing. If you tick off most of these boxes, huge congratulations! You are officially ready to start your investment journey.

# BEFORE I START INVESTING...

☐ I have deep-dived into my personal finances, created a budget, and decided how much I can afford to invest.

☐ I have decided on my money goals for the future.

☐ I have taken my pension into account and I know what it's important to consider.

☐ I understand the basics of investing.

☐ I have decided on my risk appetite and my time horizon.

☐ I have chosen a trading platform and set up an account.

☐ I have transferred the amount I want to invest into my trading account.

☐ I have researched the company/companies I want to invest in and I know when I want to sell my investment.

# Think
# sustainable

With a third of the world's wealth under our control, women are becoming richer than ever before. This shift in financial power is great news not just for women and the global economy but also for the future of our planet, because how and where we choose to place our money makes a real, tangible difference to workers and to the planet.

We have the power to make a significant change not just in our own lives but also in those of others around the world. That means when *you* have money, *you* have the power to be the change you want and have a positive impact on the world around you.

Studies show women are more than twice as likely as men to say it's very important that they buy products from companies that are ethical. But did you know that one of the most powerful ways to create societal change is not to just buy products from but actually invest in companies that are committed to creating positive impact?

This is because money equals power, so you are financially supporting and becoming an owner of a company by buying their stocks. You are giving them the power to follow their own agenda—and yours.

Interest in so-called "impact investing" or "sustainable investing" has been growing for years, but it skyrocketed during the Covid-19 pandemic, primarily driven by the large number of female investors who have rejoined the stock market. One study even found that women are willing to accept higher risk or lower return from investments in companies that have positive impacts on the world, just as women accept they must pay higher prices for rightful and ethical products.

*How and where you spend your money matters even more than how you vote.*

# Sustainable investing vs returns

When it comes to investing sustainably, investors often worry about potential performance loss. So to answer the million-dollar question: will investing with your heart sacrifice financial returns?

Let's have a look at the numbers. Morgan Stanley measured the performance of nearly 11,000 mutual funds from 2004 to 2018 and found that "there is no financial trade-off in the returns of sustainable funds compared to traditional funds." Moreover, the research even showed that in periods of high volatility, the sustainable funds were more stable. Morningstar did a similar exercise and also found that sustainability does not appear to be a drag on market-level performance. In other words, historically, you would not have got a worse financial return from investing sustainably—possibly even the contrary. This is fantastic news, because it means that using your money to support the great causes you believe in does not come at the price of diminished financial returns.

So, what's stopping you from doing good and being rewarded for doing so? Right... the how. We have talked about what to do, so let's talk about sustainable investing and see how you can align your investment portfolio with your personal values, so that you can encourage and support the impact that matters to you.

# ESG investing

When we think about sustainability, the first thing that comes to mind for most of us is our carbon footprint. But investing for impact goes way beyond environmental sustainability and can even include considerations such as gender equality, racial justice, labor equity, and firearm regulation.

To determine whether an investment is "impactful," a number of different standards are typically used. The UN's Sustainable Development Goals (or SDGs) are one example that is used by companies and governments alike. The ESG (**E**nvironmental, **S**ocial, and **G**overnance) framework is another that is often used in a corporate setting. The framework is great for categorizing companies based on how they contribute positively to society.

Let's take a closer look at each of these investigation categories: environment, social, and governance.

# E FOR ENVIRONMENT

The E measures the company's impact on our planet in terms of carbon footprint, water usage, or recycling—to name a few. It goes without saying that environmental factors are closely linked to carbon emissions, climate change, and, ultimately, quality of life for billions. Every company uses energy and resources; every company affects, and is affected by, the environment. Impact cannot be entirely avoided, but the benchmark should always be to do as little harm as possible.

# S FOR SOCIAL

The social aspect looks at the company's business relationships—such as the suppliers it uses and the values it operates within local communities. The S also includes other important aspects like labor relations, as well as diversity and human rights issues for employees.

# G FOR GOVERNANCE

Governance looks at how a company runs its business. It is the internal system of practices and procedures, the way in which the company chooses to govern itself, how it makes decisions, their legal compliance, and how well they meet the needs of external stakeholders, such as investors and governments. You could argue that governance is the most important factor, because in the end it's the management of the company that decides how sustainable and socially conscious a company wants to be, which in turn affects how well a company performs on social and environmental factors. And as governance also includes aspects such as diversity at management level, it is one criterion that cannot be overlooked.

# So, what do you do from here?

There are two options to choose from when you want to invest for sustainable impact. You can either invest directly in a company that is determined to improve their own sustainability practices, or you can invest in a company whose product itself makes a positive impact on at least one of the ESG categories. For example, you could invest in a company committed to carbon neutrality, a company working on clean water technologies, or one that is working on closing the financial gender gap.

To identify such companies, a good place to start is by investigating their own ESG reporting; if the company is truly committed, they will most likely publish their aims as well as their progress, including what ESG goals have already been achieved. This will often be published in reports—such as annual reports or specific ESG reports. (It can be a good idea to verify the company's own ESG reporting by also looking at third-party ESG ratings from professional research providers such as Sustainalytics or Morningstar, too—in the interests of staying critical!)

When analyzing how well a company is doing on their sustainability agenda, it is a great idea to compare the company's ESG goals with similar companies in the same industry. Again, this is a way of being critical toward companies that have either exaggerated the effect of their ESG efforts, or set overly ambitious and unrealistic ESG goals.

# HOW TO SPOT GREENWASHING

It is not a secret that "sustainability" is becoming an increasingly important criterion to evaluate a company's success. While this is of course a great development, unfortunately words like "carbon-neutral" or "climate-friendly" are used in marketing more than ever before—and often in false, or at least greatly exaggerated, terms. It's obvious that sustainability has become a buzzword... Everywhere we look, companies across all industries are constantly making sustainability claims in their marketing, and because these claims are so prolific it has become almost impossible to assess how true these statements actually are.

This is where the term greenwashing comes into play. Greenwashing is when a company presents itself as green—for example, via a marketing campaign that suggests their product has a positive impact on the environment—but upon closer inspection it turns out that impact is minimal or at least not as great as the claims that were made in the campaign.

Urska Trunk, Campaign Manager at Changing Markets Foundation, explains: "While brands are quick to capitalize on consumer concern by using sustainability as a marketing ploy, the vast majority of such claims are all style and no substance." In recent years, there have been countless examples of major corporations getting caught in public greenwashing scandals. One of the best things you can do to avoid falling victim to such tricks is to familiarize yourself with recent examples. Awareness will help you notice red flags when things look too good to be true.

# HOW CAN YOU AVOID GREENWASHING?

It's easy to get scammed by elaborate marketing ploys of large companies. That's because it's extremely difficult to spot greenwashing and even more difficult to determine if a company is actually doing what they say they are in terms of sustainability. There are, however, a few things you can look out for:

- **Vague claims of sustainability**, such as "climate-friendly," which you can't easily find documentation for, are usually a red flag. Research how the company backs up their claims and look into the credibility of the information. If you can't find the answers easily, you often already have your answer. But also try asking the company directly, and if you still don't get answers you can draw your own conclusions, given the lack of transparency.
- **Single considerations and initiatives for sustainability** don't make it a sustainable product. A typical example is claiming the packaging of a product is made out of recycled material, while the product itself still contains many environmentally harmful substances.
- **Companies' own labels for sustainability** are something to look out for. It could be an e-commerce site that has designed their own sustainability label. Research the label, and find out what it actually says about the product.

**Using your money to support the great causes you believe in does not come at the price of diminished financial returns.**

# European disclosure regulation

One factor making ESG-investing complicated is that there are no global regulations or definitions for what makes something sustainable. Instead, it's up to each individual investor to decide for themselves what practices, values, and ESG goals are most important in a company or fund. However, progress is being made! Europe is spearheading this change with a new disclosure regulation for all European funds.

The regulation is called SFDR, which stands for "Sustainable Finance Disclosure Regulation." Don't let the dry and boring name scare you off, because this is great news for all who want to invest in sustainable funds. This SFDR regulation will enhance transparency on just how sustainable a specific fund is. This means that all investors wanting to put money into a European investment fund now have a tool they can use to compare different funds, so they can easily evaluate how sustainable the fund is in order to make an informed decision.

All funds within the EU have to be categorized within three different levels of sustainability, so if you are interested in investing in sustainable funds, looking to Europe is definitely helpful. Most major trading platforms will allow you to buy European funds, even if you're not based in the region.

The regulation scheme works using a scale of 1 to 3 in terms of meeting sustainability criteria—just with slightly more complicated names for the funds, including article 6, article 8, and article 9. So, here's what they all mean, and what you should be looking out for.

**Article 6:** Funds in this category offer the lowest level of sustainability. Article 6 funds have very few sustainability considerations when deciding what investments are to be included in them.

**Article 8:** One step up from article 6 are article 8 funds. These have set up specific criteria for environmental and social practices within the fund. This means that certain sectors or companies that harm the environment might be excluded, such as oil and gas, tobacco, etc.

**Article 9:** At the highest level, you have funds categorized as article 9. In these funds, sustainability is integrated as a goal in the investment strategy. The fund is not only screening out certain sectors or companies but choosing to include companies that are the best in their class in terms of sustainability.

## SFDR REGULATION CODES TO LOOK OUT FOR

**ARTICLE 9**

In these funds, sustainability is integrated as a goal in the investment strategy

**ARTICLE 8**

These funds have set up specific criteria for environmental and social practices within the fund

**ARTICLE 6**

These funds have very few sustainability considerations when deciding what investments are included in the fund

HIGH — FOCUS ON SUSTAINABILITY — LOW

# HOW DO YOU FIND THIS INFORMATION?

Knowing that article 9 is the highest score for sustainability practices, you might be eager to start researching funds asap. This information will be accessible on the trading platform on the fund's page, but if it's not highlighted, you should be able to find it in the prospectus of the fund or in the annual report.

Of course, the SFDR regulation only applies to funds set up in the EU. If you're looking to invest in, for example, a North American or Asian fund, unfortunately you won't be able to find this method of ranking yet.

On a positive note, more and more companies are also working hard to limit their negative impact on our planet, which is an effort that's definitely worth supporting.

Here are a few examples of companies who, in different ways, have tried to implement sustainable practices, even though they may still have areas left for improvement. (Please note: This is not given as investment advice!)

# 1 Beyond Meat

Did you know that 18% of global greenhouse emissions are created by animal agriculture? That's why Beyond Meat has created plant-based meat substitutes to limit the carbon footprint of the meat industry. Besides selling meat substitutes to the likes of Walmart and McDonald's, the brand recently overhauled packaging design to significantly reduce waste.

# 2 Chipotle Mexican Grill

In 2022 the company announced that up to 15% of its officers' annual incentives will be tied to their progress toward achieving the company's sustainability and diversity goals. (Similar initiatives have also been announced by McDonald's and Starbucks.) The company even plans to release its carbon emissions footprint four years ahead of schedule.

# 3 Ørsted

Long before it was a hot topic or even profitable, Denmark's national oil and gas company (at that time called DONG Energy) made a radical shift from being almost 100% fossil fuel–based to now being almost 100% renewable energy–based. In less than 10 years the company has successfully stopped all oil and gas activities and are now the world leader in producing green electricity from offshore wind turbines.

# 4 Patagonia

Although not publicly traded—and therefore not a company that can be invested in—we still think it deserves a mention on this list. By encouraging customers not to buy more Patagonia clothing, donating to organizations fighting climate change and participating in 1% for the Planet— giving 1% of their sales back to the environment every year—Patagonia is so much more than a clothing brand.

**PERNILLE**

# "Simple living and sustainable investing."

Since starting her investing journey 20 years ago, Pernille has made it her mission to educate others on the importance of sustainable investing. As an author, coach and mentor in investing, Pernille has the philosophy that replacing overconsumption with simplicity is the first step toward financial freedom.

**Sustainability as a conscious choice:** Sustainable investing has been a journey for me over the last 20 years. When I started, I focused on growing my money as much as possible, but when I had my children, 15 years ago, it really opened my eyes to sustainability, and this has been my focus ever since.

**Ask yourself: is there a future for this?** When I pick investments, the first thing I look for is the product. Is this something I see a future for? Is it something that can help push the world in a better direction? I firmly believe that the best investments are the sustainable ones, as it's the sustainable companies that are here to stay. I also think of sustainability in a broader sense—looking into how the company treats employees and the surrounding community.

**It doesn't come without dilemmas:** Sustainable investing comes with its own set of problems and I myself have invested in companies that I can see today were not very sustainable. Particularly, local pollution and employee conditions in China concern me. As consumers and shareholders, we can use our power to make these corporations act more sustainably. I usually look into the company's annual report to see whether it is trying to make itself greener, in addition to providing a product or service that's inherently green. If a company isn't sustainable in its practices, then it's not necessarily a sustainable investment in the long term.

**Limit overconsumption and start small:** If you don't overconsume, you live more cheaply. And if you then spend the money you save on investing, your wealth increases faster. I personally saved money by living a simpler life and buying as few new things as possible.

# Four steps to start investing sustainably

Hopefully by now we have convinced you that investing sustainably is a win-win situation for your own finances and for the world at large, because, remember, the moment you buy a stock of a company or participate in a fund or ETF, you are an owner of those companies! But how do you actually do it? Below is an easy-to-follow guide covering four steps to think about before you start investing:

1. Value alignment: What is important to you?
2. Investment options: How do you want to invest—in a single company or a fund?
3. Research: Where and for what do you need to look?
4. Diversification check-up: How do you ensure that you are diversified enough?

# 01 VALUE ALIGNMENT

The first thing you need to do is figure out what matters to you. There's no one-size-fits-all solution here, everyone is different and everyone has different values. When looking at the ESG factors, what is the most important aspect that *you* want to put your money into? Is it clean energy? Is it women in leadership? Or perhaps it's something else entirely. Knowing your priorities and values is key, as it lays the groundwork for your personal strategy. You need to know what you're looking for in order not to be overwhelmed by endless options. But as is the case with any investments, a healthy diversification should always be considered.

## Action

Make a list of three focus points or a set of rules—for example, start with "the company must...." Use these as a guide and make a note of them, as you'll need to turn to these for step three, the research phase.

# 02 CONSIDER INVESTMENT OPTIONS

Step two of your sustainable investing journey is to consider your investment options. If you're already investing you'll first need to do a portfolio clean up. Revisit your current portfolio and look at the considerations from step one. See if you need to remove any stocks or funds that no longer match your values. Of course, don't just blindly sell them, but prepare to remove them from your portfolio in the long term, when the time is right.

After that, consider what type of investment you want. Are you looking at buying single stocks or are you leaning toward funds?

You can create your own ethical portfolio by buying stocks yourself that you feel are aligned with your beliefs and values. Alternatively, you can find an investment fund that screens out unethical companies and looks at the best, most socially responsible investments.

# 03 RESEARCH

This is the biggest and most important step! You now know what you're looking for. You've decided what investment type you are interested in buying and you have prepared a list of values. Awesome! You're on the right track. Next up is research.

We've divided this step into two parts—the first is for buying single stocks, the second is for buying funds. Once we've got through that we'll share our best tips for doing due diligence for both.

## IF YOU'RE BUYING SINGLE STOCKS FROM A COMPANY

Look at your list of ESG values (see page 139). Decide on one key element on which you want to base your research. For instance, let's say you want to focus on environmental factors—the E—and, more specifically, you want to invest in a company offering a product that reduces carbon emissions. You have various options for researching here:

- **Do a Google search.** Really this is the best way to start the research phase. Go to Google; type in "green energy technology stocks" or "renewable energy stocks." Different companies and sectors might show up, such as solar energy or wind power. You might also find articles like "Ten green companies to invest in" from big financial institutions or other media. Use such articles to find inspiration, but remember to be critical! Then it's time to be more specific—such as "solar companies + country or region" (Scandinavia, Asia, US... etc.).
- **Action:** Take notes or bookmark interesting companies in your browser.

- **Ask your network.** Try asking around in your own network of friends, family, or colleagues. You might be surprised by their insights or ideas.
- **Look at sustainable funds.** Another tactic could be to look into the companies that are included in sustainable investment funds. Look at the prospectus of the fund and go to the list of companies it includes. This is a good place to start when you're a little unsure of what is out there.
- **Action:** Write down 10–15 companies to research further.
- **Listen to podcasts.** If you're not a fan of reading, try looking into the podcast offerings available. You could do a quick search in your preferred app. Usually the different podcasts use keywords or tags for their episodes, making it easier to find relevant options.

## IF YOU WANT TO INVEST IN A SUSTAINABLE FUND

Sustainable investment funds have become very popular in recent years. This is great news for private investors as we now have a much wider range of investment options than before. But as with any investment decision, the struggle is to figure out which one is the right fit for you. The ultimate goal would be a fund that matches your values 100%—however, that might be difficult to find. Let's take a look at what you can do to help find the one for you:

- **Do a Google search.** Look at your list of values from step one and type in "Sustainable Funds for women CEOs"—you might find that several sites mention the same funds as an investment option.
- **Action:** Write down a list of 5–10 funds that look interesting and are aligned with your values. Make notes for each or bookmark the websites.

- **Apply filters on the trading platform.** Go to the trading platform where you usually make your investments and head to the exchange page. Often you will have the option to apply different filters, to screen the funds. On many platforms it's even possible to apply a "sustainability filter," where you can further narrow down the options.
- **Action:** Add any interesting funds to your list, or bookmark them.
- **Listen to podcasts.** As before, do a quick search in your preferred app for relevant subjects.

Once you have done your broad research for stocks and/or funds, look at your notes, your list of companies, and your values. With the information you have now gleaned, narrow down the list to five options.

# Due diligence

Now it's time to do your due diligence. Take your list of the five companies or funds that you ended up with and follow the guide below.

## SINGLE STOCKS FROM COMPANIES

We always say: Never invest in something you don't understand. This goes for sustainable investing, too. You should establish how the company operates—beyond its sustainability agenda. So, research the business model—how the company makes money. If you don't understand this after researching it, simply don't invest. For example, if a company claims to sell a product that produces 90% fewer emissions than competitive products and sells it at a third of the price, you have to make sure you understand the business model—even if their sustainable agenda might appear to be flawless.

Secondly, research their ESG goals and the value you've decided is your focus. Use these five questions as inspiration:

1. Does the company have a specific ESG budget?
2. Are there formal procurement and supply-chain ethical standards in place, including making sure that modern slavery does not occur in the supply chains?

3. Do circular (self-repairing) economy principles, origin of resources and/or sustainable, or local sourcing feature in its procurement policies?
4. Does the company publish its greenhouse gas emissions reports and its achievement of its greenhouse gas emissions reduction targets?
5. What does the company regard as the most important sustainability issues that its business faces?

You will often be able to find the necessary information on the company's website. Look at the company's goals and, based on the knowledge you have now, consider if you believe they are realistic. Try comparing the goals with those of another similar company (in terms of size, country, and industry). Did your initial company set overambitious ESG goals compared to the other company and is there a good reason why?

The final thing to do from here is to look at how the company has been rated by a third-party institution.

- You can use Sustainalytics' rating tool to look up different companies and see their ESG rating or Morningstar's sustainability rating.
- You could also try to see if the company is a certified B Corp, which is the highest accreditation a company can get within sustainability.

# B CORP

If you really want to support sustainability through investment, companies with B Corp Certification should be at the top of your list. This designation is given to businesses that meet very high standards of verified performance, accountability, and transparency on factors from employee benefits and charitable giving to supply chain practices and input materials.

In order to achieve certification, a company must:

- Demonstrate high social and environmental performance.
- Make a legal commitment by changing their corporate governance structure to be accountable to all stakeholders—not just shareholders.
- Exhibit transparency by allowing information about their performance and sustainability practices to be publicly available.

When looking at all the research, critically evaluate if the company lives up to your standards and aligns with your values.

So, you've done the groundwork, now here is your due diligence checklist:

☐ I understand how the company operates, what the product is and its business model (how it makes money).

☐ I know what their ESG goals are and have critically evaluated these goals.

☐ I have compared the company's goals with those of similar companies from the same industry and size in order to better determine if the goals are realistic.

☐ I have done basic research on their website and their annual report.

☐ I have looked at the company's ratings from a third-party source.

# Investment funds

When you have identified a handful of interesting funds, it's time to take a closer look at them. Ideally, you would have to go through all companies included in the fund using the above list. However, this would require you to spend days on research. If you're up for that—go for it! But honestly, most of us would start and not finish.

There are different ways of getting around this struggle. You could decide to research the companies that form the greatest percentage of the fund—for example, the ten biggest companies within it. Of course, this approach is not as accurate as doing the full research of all the companies included. In the end, how far you go is up to you and depends on how much time you have available and that you're willing to invest in the process.

If the fund tracks an index, look at the index—what sectors and companies does it include?

Then look at third-party ratings of the five funds on your list. Here are some easy ways to do this:

- Use Morningstar's sustainability screener.
- Also you can look at www.asyousow.org if you want to check what the fund is investing in (not all funds are included, unfortunately).
- For gender-lens investing or equality investing, try looking up the fund on www.genderequalityfunds.org.

If you're looking at a European fund, remember that you can look at their SFDR rating (see page 132). If the fund is categorized as article 9, that's the highest rating it can get, whereas an article 6 fund is the lowest-scoring in regards to ESG.

Right, so now you're left with a certain number of options for funds. It could be three, it could be one. Either way—great work! Bring the list to the next step, which is the diversification check-up.

## Action

Cross out the funds on your list that didn't make the cut when doing the due diligence.

# 04 DIVERSIFICATION CHECK-UP

The last step before heading to the trading platform to hit the buy button is to do a portfolio check-up.

Look at the stock or fund you're planning on buying. How does it sit with the rest of your portfolio? You need to make sure that your portfolio remains sufficiently diversified after adding the new investment to it. This is especially relevant if you're buying stocks from a company. If you already have an investment fund, see if the company is included in your existing fund.

In general, investment funds offer higher diversification because they include many different companies. However, if the fund only includes companies from a specific country or sector (for example, an index fund tracking the performance of the biggest tech companies), you should pay attention to this in regards to diversification.

Use this as an opportunity to critically go through your portfolio and see if the company, and the sector it belongs to is a good match in terms of diversification. Perhaps you're invested in this specific sector already? Are you too focused on one geographical region? Are too many of your investments into small and therefore highly-speculative companies?

If everything looks great, you're ready for the next step—buying! So let's get down to business...

*Money is power—power to change our future, and power to make the world a better place for all. We don't have to choose between the two.*

# 5

# Making your first investment

Now we've got here, even with everything you've learned, pressing the buy button and making your first investment might seem terrifying, but in reality buying a stock is no different from buying any other item on the internet.

Over the following pages, we'll guide you through all the steps and share some strategies that can help guide you to the *right* investment.

# WHAT TO BUY

When it comes to making your first investment, deciding what to buy might seem like an overwhelming task, so on the following pages we are proposing three strategies, all of which are well suited for new investors. Even though these are all different, they do have two things in common: They are long term, and they revolve around diversification. Let's recap on why that is:

## INVESTING FOR THE LONG RUN

No one knows what will happen next week, month, or year; it's impossible to predict the future, and it's also impossible to predict how the market will develop in the short term. Therefore, having a long time horizon is key. In this book, a long time horizon refers to a period of at least five years, but preferably longer, which means you keep your money invested for at least five years. Of course, this means you need to be able to manage your finances without this money for that period of time.

## DIVERSIFICATION

As explained throughout this book, diversification is a prerequisite for becoming a successful long-term investor; the more options you have, the better the results. So don't play it safe by putting your money into just one source, spread out your investments to balance out peaks and troughs across the global markets.

If this seems overwhelming, to make it easy for you, we've outlined four ways to diversify your portfolio:

1.  Invest across different continents and industries: That way it won't negatively impact your entire portfolio if something happens on one continent or industry.
2.  Invest across asset types: Diversification doesn't just refer to investing in different stocks, it also refers to investing in different asset classes, such as commodities or real estate.
3.  Avoid home-country bias: When choosing stocks, a common mistake among investors is to have a home-country bias, which means they mainly invest in companies they know about from local news. This approach creates an overrepresentation of stocks from the home country, which increases the overall risk.
4.  Include mutual funds in your investment mix: Many investors find it intimidating to hand-pick 10 or more stocks from different countries and industries. If you recognize this feeling, mutual funds might be for you (see page 97). By investing in just one fund, you indirectly invest in all the businesses within that fund.

# Did you know?

A study by Fidelity found that women aged 18–35 now begin investing at the average age of 21. By contrast, women currently aged 36 and older started investing when they were 30 on average. That's a difference of nine years, which is clear evidence that women are increasingly taking on the world of investing and breaking down the financial gender divides.

# Monkeys at Wall Street outperformed professional bankers

Are you worried you don't know enough about investing to pick the right stocks? And does this fear keep you from getting started? Then keep on reading, you'll love this study.

The story starts in 1973 when people used to read the newspaper, and each newspaper would report pages about stocks. A professor at Princeton University, Burton Malkiel, had just released a book called *A Random Walk Down Wall Street*. A famous sentence in the book reads, "A blindfolded monkey throwing darts at a newspaper's financial pages could select a portfolio that would do just as well as one carefully selected by experts."

A company called Research Affiliates decided to test this claim. To do so, they randomly selected 100 portfolios containing 30 stocks from a 1,000 stock universe. They repeated this process every year, from 1964 to 2010, and tracked the results. The process replicated 100 monkeys throwing darts at the stock pages each year.

The results were astounding; because the "monkey" portfolios performed better 98% of the time, showing that a monkey with no technical knowledge can outperform the market consistently.

Moral of the story? You don't need a fancy degree or an expensive suit to make money on the stock market.

# Three evergreen strategies

There are many options for choosing an investment strategy. For most people, building a solid portfolio is a tricky art to master. But contrary to how it might sound, an investment strategy doesn't have to be complicated when you understand the basics of risk and time horizons (see page 101).

Here we'll introduce three strategies that are well-suited for new investors. Once you've read them and decided on a strategy, staying cool is key. This means *not* changing your strategy as soon as the market fluctuates slightly, because it is important to remember that these fluctuations are often temporary. By sticking with your plan, you avoid making irrational decisions based on fear or greed. However, if your overall financial situation changes, it might be a good idea to adapt your strategy and risk profile accordingly.

## BUY-AND-HOLD

The buy-and-hold strategy is very simple: You pick an investment, buy it, then hold on to it for years. Even though this sounds simple, many investors find it difficult to sit tight and leave their investments alone. No matter how experienced you are, large market fluctuations always make up a tempting opportunity to over-trade. But remember, by the time you read the news about a specific investment, 99% of other investors have already heard that news and the market has reacted.

The buy-and-hold strategy revolves around the idea that "time in the market" is better than "timing the market." In this way you stay invested no matter what, because you believe that long-term returns will be worth the short-term volatility. This passive approach is essentially the opposite of trying to "beat the market," where you trade on a regular basis in the hope of getting better returns than the rest of the market. If you are considering this approach, here are a few pros and cons to help you make your decision:

 **Pros**
- **It works:** This strategy has been proven over and over again to give exponential gains on invested capital.
- **It's easy:** Once you've built your portfolio, you won't need to make changes or check prices.
- **It's cheap:** Because you trade less, there'll be fewer transactions and you'll pay less in commission and fees, which can make a big difference to your long-term investment returns.

 **Cons**
- **It ties up capital:** Potentially this approach has a large opportunity cost, because your capital is tied up for long periods of time, during which you may miss out on other opportunities.
- **It takes time to see results:** This strategy relies on the magic of compound interest (see page 105), which requires patience.
- **It's tough during crashes:** You may face big losses during economic downturns, because you won't sell your investments even if they continue to drop for some time.

# DOLLAR-COST AVERAGING

How do you buy when prices are low and sell when they are high?

The short answer is: You can't always. Again, predicting the stock market is impossible, and no one knows what the future holds. Therefore, it's all about getting a nice average price and avoiding investing all your money at the peak. One way of doing that is by investing gradually, which is also known as dollar-cost averaging.

When using this strategy, you invest smaller amounts of money at different points in time rather than investing all your money at once. There is no rule for how long it should be between each investment or how much you need to invest each time. Also, it's up to you whether you keep investing in the same thing or buy different things each time. You can even have an automatic transaction that invests your money every month, so you don't need to perform the trades manually when you're busy getting on with other things.

By investing at all times of the market cycle, you smooth out the peaks and troughs created by market volatility. At the same time, you also allow yourself to expand the mix of your portfolio and diversify even more over time. In this way, the strategy aligns with the notion that investing is an ongoing discipline, which you need to nurture. As you make more money, you should keep investing on a regular basis. Remember: Rome wasn't built in a day, and neither is your portfolio.

*Let's take an example here...*

You have $300, which you want to invest over three months, investing $100 each time. If you want to buy a stock that costs $20 per share you'd be able to purchase five shares in one month for $100. The next month, when you have another $100 to invest, the price increases to $50 per share, so you'd be able to purchase only two shares. Next month, the price drops to $10 per share and you could buy 10 shares. You therefore end up getting 17 shares for $300 and your average cost per share is $17.6 ($300 ÷ 17 = $17.6). Here's a breakdown:

| Time | Amount invested | Share price in the market | Number of shares bought that month | Total shares |
|---|---|---|---|---|
| Month 1 | $100 | $20 | 5 | 5 |
| Month 2 | $100 | $50 | 2 | 7 |
| Month 3 | $100 | $10 | 10 | 17 |

Is this good or bad? Well, that depends how the market develops. If you had invested all your money in month three at $10 per share you would have got a better deal. But if you had invested everything in month two at $50 per share, you would have paid a higher price and therefore got a smaller return. This shows how the dollar-cost average strategy protects you from investing everything at the peak and gives you a nice average price.

Once more, there are pros and cons to this strategy that you might want to consider before committing to it:

 **Pros**

- **It's great if your risk tolerance is low:** If risk makes you uncomfortable and you get nervous about market volatility, this strategy helps you stay consistent and removes fear, because the purpose is to get a nice average price rather than buying at the perfect time.
- **It allows you to start with small amounts:** If you don't have much money to invest, this strategy helps you get started with small amounts and build wealth over time.

 **Cons**

- **It can be expensive:** As you trade more frequently, you will also need to pay more fees to your trading platform.
- **You might miss out on profit:** Because markets tend to go up over time, you might miss out on good returns by investing small amounts over a period of time rather than investing a bigger amount early on.

# CORE-SATELLITE STRATEGY

The core-satellite strategy is based on the concept that 80% of your portfolio should be a "core" of low-risk diversified investments, while the last 20% should be riskier investments ("satellites"). The idea behind this is to create a foundation of "safer" investments following the average market, while the satellites add an extra layer of risk and thereby potential for greater profit or loss.

Here's an explanation of what we mean:

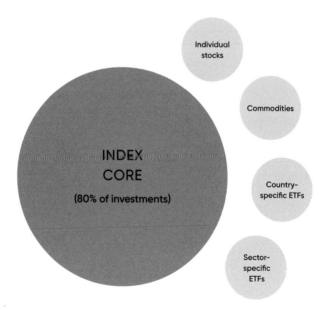

## THE CORE

The "core" refers to having a diversified foundation of investments as described in the buy-and-hold strategy (see page 155). This should be a mix of different investments, such as mutual funds or ETFs, which act as the foundation of your portfolio. They might not be the most exciting of performers, but they'll help steady the ship.

## THE SATELLITES

The satellites represent the riskier investments, which are each chosen based on their individual potential. Satellites could be stocks or funds that are riskier on their own but when combined with your core of less-risky investment will even out your portfolio. The core-satellite strategy allows you to add a personal touch to your strategy while benefiting from the average market return. It also allows you to manage risk, which you can turn up and down as you prefer, and gives you the opportunity to be more involved and engaged with your investments if you're the type of investor who easily gets bored with the buy-and-hold strategy. However, this strategy could be viewed as a riskier version of buy-and-hold, as the only difference is the 20% satellites.

### Pros

- **It allows for a personal touch:** By adding a personal touch to your portfolio you reduce FOMO on new trends or niche areas you are interested in.
- **You can adjust risk:** If you take a risk and it doesn't work out, you've only allocated a small portion of your portfolio towards it and so have minimized your loss. Therefore, you can try out different investment approaches without jeopardizing all your money.

### Cons

- **It does not have a great track record:** Unfortunately, investors trying to beat the market have a long history of failing. So even though the satellites around the core can potentially improve return, history suggests most investors will fail to do so.
- **It can be expensive:** You will most likely trade the satellites more frequently than the core, and you will therefore also need to pay more fees to your trading platform.

*This strategy does what it says it will do: It builds a core of long-term diversified investments surrounded by riskier satellites.*

# Three steps to make your first trade

Once you've decided on a strategy, it's time to get moving and make your first trade. Even though it might seem like a small action, this represents a major milestone, because once you've made your first trade, making the second, third, and fourth trades is much easier. This is the moment when you're finally taking charge of your financial future.

**1**

### Create a trading account
In order to invest, you need to create a trading account. This account gives you access to the stock market, and you create it on a trading platform.

## FIVE THINGS TO CONSIDER WHEN CHOOSING A TRADING PLATFORM

Depending on the country, you will find that there are different trading platforms to choose from. Often there will be a couple of market leaders to consider. A simple Google search can be a good way to get a quick overview of the options. Then once you have done some research, you can start to compare the trading platforms before you make your choice...

1. **Fees**
   This is an important consideration, as costs and fees can really eat away your final return. These can include cost per trade, annual fees, withdrawal fees, and bid offer spreads—where a commission is taken on the difference between purchase and sale. The relevance of these will depend on the amount of funds you'll invest and likely frequency of trading.

2. **Investment options available**
   Are their stocks and shares locally based or is there global access? Do they trade in funds? Some platforms offer a huge range while others have specialized funds only. Do they have sustainability ranking?

3. **User-friendliness**
   Is it available in your local country? How user-friendly is the account? Do you find it easy to navigate or is it overly complex? Can you access the platform from your desktop or do they offer an app?

4. **Reputation**
   How long has the trading platform been around? Is it listed on a stock exchange? This is important for the protection of your money if, in a very rare situation, a platform stops doing business.

5. **Demo and support**
   Can you take advantage of a demo account to mimic the trades with the platform before you start? Is there customer support available online or on the phone in case you have any issues?

As a rule of thumb, traditional banks are usually more expensive and less user-friendly than the newer neobanks. Unlike traditional banks, neobanks offer banking services that are strictly online, and they are known to challenge the traditional banks by offering cheaper and better services to the average person. Of course, there can be exceptions, so you need to do your own research before choosing. It's also good to know that all trading platforms are highly regulated by the financial authorities. The likelihood of getting scammed is extremely small if you go with a reputable broker, but always do your research beforehand.

**Transfer money**

Once you've created a trading account you need to transfer money into it. But how much money should you invest? This is probably the question we get asked the most, and the answer is... "it depends." It depends on the trading fees, your strategy, and your financial situation. It is commonly said that you can get started for a few hundred dollars, depending on the fees on your platform. As a rule of thumb, you can get started with small amounts down to $100 as long as the fees don't make up more than 0.5% of the overall investment.

**Invest**

You are now ready to make your first investment! It goes as follows:

1. Type the name of the stock/fund/ETF you wish to purchase in the search bar.
2. State *"amount"* and *"price."*
   - ◆ **Amount:** How many stocks you wish to purchase.
   - ◆ **Price:** The price you are willing to pay. Usually this is what the stock was traded for most recently, which appears on the trading platform. If you wish to purchase the stock at a lower price, you have to wait for a seller willing to sell at that price, which may take longer (and might not happen at all).
3. Click "buy."

Once you press buy your order is in the market and it will be completed once someone decides to sell. Large-cap stocks usually have many buyers and sellers, and it typically only takes seconds or minutes for a trade to go through. Small-cap stocks, on the other hand, often have fewer investors, so it might take longer for the trade to go through. The stock will appear in your account as soon as the trade is complete.

# NOW...

# GROWTH

# 6

# Managing your investment portfolio

You've done it! You've joined the growing ranks of women who are taking control of their finances, getting involved in the world of investments, and embarking on a journey towards financial freedom. So, what's next? How do you build on this and maintain your investments to build the future you deserve?

Making your first investments is just the start of your journey toward financial freedom. In order to truly succeed in the long term, you need to be consistent and manage your portfolio carefully. Luckily for you, the initial investment is a much bigger mental step than managing it afterward.

Expect ups and downs along the road—it's a natural part of the process. In this last section of the book, we will touch upon how to deal with market volatility, sharing the most important dos and don'ts of managing your portfolio during times of economic uncertainty, and how to stay calm in the process.

# You've started investing— now what?

You're now ready for the easy part of investing: waiting. As we've repeatedly said throughout this book, investing is a long-term game and you should always *invest and wait* rather than *wait to invest*. However, your portfolio might need a few adjustments along the way.

## QUARTERLY DROP-IN

You should aim to sit down with your portfolio once every three months. Although this might not sound very frequent, you actually want to avoid checking your portfolio manically twice a day—obsessive overchecking will not only take a toll on your job, social life, and crucial Netflix habit, it will also cause you to become more susceptible to the biggest investor threats: fear and greed. If you watch your stock's value plummet, you'll become scared and inclined to sell, and you might even make rash decisions. If you ride out the waves, you're much more likely to make long-term gains. That's why three-month check-ins are sufficient to stay updated about your investments without being obsessive.

# MAJOR CHANGES ALERT

That said, it is worth keeping your eyes open to changes, whether they're specific to the stock or fund that you're holding, or in a wider economic sense. A top tip is to have a Google alert set up so that any news relating to your stocks of interest will neatly slide into your inbox. This isn't necessarily an alert to make you drop everything and go straight to your portfolio and sell up, but it does keep you informed so that you can understand your portfolio well and make proper, considered decisions.

# PRE-DECIDED WITHDRAWAL

Before you made your first investment you should already have decided roughly when you were going to sell it. Forward planning is a must! This forms part of your investment strategy and is another line of defense against fear and greed. When setting a deadline, make sure you have flexibility around it; this will allow you to adapt if the market experiences volatility around your desired selling time.

# ANNUAL REBALANCE

As discussed on page 104, five years is the minimum time horizon to have in your mind before embarking upon buying stocks and shares. With this timeframe, sitting down once a year for a fully comprehensive assessment of your investments is more than sufficient. Structure your meeting with yourself and your portfolio around the following five points:

1.   What am I looking to buy next?
2.   What, if anything, might need selling?
3.   How geographically diverse are my holdings?
4.   Do I hold enough sectors in my portfolio?
5.   Is my portfolio still diversified, or are some investments taking up too much space?

Keep up the research and make informing yourself a habit; whether it's through reading relevant articles, listening to podcasts, or watching videos and media. And just remember, historically you would've made more in the 10 days after a market drop than at any other time over the last 50 years. Managing your portfolio is super important, but more than anything, managing your emotions is crucial.

The end of the calendar year, at least in the Northern Hemisphere, is typically wet and cold, so what better time to grab a big mug of something hot and set in for a solid appointment with yourself to plan your end of year portfolio? Easily said, but how do you go about this and what do you need to consider?

# BUDGET

First things first: Assess your ins, outs, and budgets. It might be that you've moved places and your rent has gone up, meaning there's less available to spend—and less to save. Alternatively, you might have done a damn good job at work and been given a well-deserved promotion and pay rise, suddenly giving you excess cash that you've not quite worked out what to do with—other than spend it on more takeaways. Take stock, and see if the budget you had set is working for you now and if you're saving enough for Future You.

# ACCOUNTS

Have you opened or closed some or any of your trading platforms or bank accounts in the year? Have these sites altered their charges or rates on your savings? While they might have been good choices when you first opened them, situations can change, sometimes making you an incompatible match. Don't be afraid to shop around for something better, and consider consolidating accounts where possible.

Remember, you are the customer and you can set demands or switch providers as you wish. Being in the driver's seat is important in every aspect of your financial journey, and choosing a trading platform is no different.

# Investment performance

Now it's time for the nitty-gritty. Who were the winners and who didn't pull through over the last 12 months? Most importantly, why was this? If you can work out what has occurred, it will help you to look ahead and work out if the investment still has a place in your financial strategy in the long term, or whether it's time to move on.

Additionally, the make-up of your portfolio should always be diverse, as you'd hopefully set out for it to be when planning what to invest in. However, if a stock or share has grown considerably, it might be taking up a much larger chunk of your portfolio than you had initially imagined. You'll need to work out what the potential drawbacks of this could be in your portfolio and how to balance this out if it looks like it is going to be a problem.

# TAX AND ADMIN

Hopefully you should have a good grasp of what the last year has delivered for you and you'll now be able to whiz through any relevant tax returns and admin that's required. It might be that you don't need to do this until a later, specified date, but it never hurts to prepare. At this point, it might also be worth flicking back to your investments to check out if you can offset any losses with gains and make the most of any tax allowances you're entitled to.

# GOAL SETTING

While you're setting your personal new year's resolutions you should do the same for your portfolio and budget. Are you expecting any bonuses or changes to your available investment budget in the next year? Based on last year's performance of your investments, in which areas do you anticipate seeing gains? Do you need to think about introducing any new investments or adjusting your contributions to a certain savings area? Be realistic and stay strong in your strategy by setting out your portfolio goals for the year ahead.

# Navigating market volatility

Have you ever looked at your investments to find they have suddenly plummeted, only to see them bounce back a few weeks later? Then you're not alone. No matter what you invest in, the value of your investments will fluctuate over time. However, there's a difference between seeing fluctuations of individual investments and fluctuations of the entire market, also known as market volatility.

So what is volatility? This is an investment term that describes when a market or security experiences periods of unpredictable, and sometimes sharp, price movements. People often think about volatility only when prices fall—however, volatility can also refer to sudden price rises.

The stock market is affected by many different factors, all of which can lead to volatility. Two key factors are:

- *The global economy.* When the global economy slows down, consumers decrease their spending and business activity decreases as well. As a result, the stock market decreases in value. The global economy is also affected by big events such as the outbreak of Covid-19, political events, or natural disasters.
- *Investor psychology.* Investors tend to confirm each other's beliefs in both positive and negative scenarios when it comes to how a stock, sector, or even the market in general is expected to perform. Because investors aren't always rational, this factor can be difficult to predict.

# HOW SHOULD YOU HANDLE VOLATILITY?

During volatile times, many investors get spooked and begin to question their long-term investment strategy. This especially happens for new investors who are often tempted to sell their investments and wait on the sidelines until it seems safe to dive back in.

However, it's important to understand that market volatility is inevitable and that the very nature of the stock market is volatile in the short term. Therefore, always keep a long time horizon. Does that sound easy? Well, it isn't. Because investing often involves a lot of emotions, and the higher the volatility, the higher the risk and the more of an emotional roller-coaster you will experience!

# KNOW YOUR RISK APPETITE

Perhaps this is a good occasion to ask yourself if your current level of risk is the right fit for you? Are you anxious and awake at night worrying about your stocks? If so, you may want to consider lowering your risk and slowly transitioning into more dependable investments.

*No matter what you invest in, the value of your investments will fluctuate over time.*

# REMEMBER, IT'S A LONG GAME

It is not easy to navigate uncertainty. (Honestly, we lean toward the strategy of not even opening our trading accounts during extreme volatility, because we are in it for the long term, so it doesn't actually matter what happens today, tomorrow, or even a year from now.) But one thing that always works to help us stay calm and avoid panic selling is reminding ourselves of historical data. Remember that the global stock market has increased 7–10% every year—and this includes all those years with crises such as the IT bubble and the housing crisis.

# VOLATILITY IS AN OPPORTUNITY

Volatility is not always a bad thing, because market corrections can sometimes provide attractive opportunities for investment. If you have cash and are waiting to invest in the stock market, a market correction can provide an opportunity to do so at a lower price. If you already own stocks, downward market volatility could also be an attractive opportunity to buy additional shares in companies you believe will perform well in the long run. By understanding volatility and its causes, investors can potentially take advantage of the investment opportunities that it provides to generate better long-term returns.

*Let's take an example:*
Following a drop in stock prices, Selina can buy for $50 a share that was worth $100 a short time before. Buying shares in this way lowers the average cost-per-share, which helps to improve her portfolio's performance when the markets eventually rebound.

The process is the same when a share rises quickly. Selina can then take advantage by selling out and investing the profit in other areas she believes offer better opportunities.

# DON'T PANIC

The number one rule when market volatility hits is to stay calm and not let panic push you into making a rash decision. Volatility can be scary and many fear great loss when they see their investments start to drop, but over time, market volatility wears off and prices should increase.

Markets fluctuate over time, but one of the biggest mistakes investors make is trying to time the market; trying to guess the "best" time to buy and sell, to get the best possible return. Don't make that mistake, because time in the market beats timing the market—in other words, if you invest consistently and start early, history suggests you will get a better return.

Another mistake investors make is that, when markets are in a downturn, most investors want to do something—act! The explanation? Well, we're human. We are designed to act when faced with danger. Some freeze, some flee, usually without careful consideration... And that's why sticking to your strategy is always the best decision.

# Summing up

- Market volatility is inevitable: It's the nature of the markets to move up and down over the short term.
- Volatile markets are usually characterized by large price fluctuations and increased trading activity.
- One way to deal with volatility is to avoid it altogether; this means staying invested for the long term and not paying attention to short-term fluctuations.

As business magnate and investor Warren Buffet famously said: "Be fearful when others are greedy and greedy when others are fearful."

*You worked hard for your money. Now it's time to let your money work for you.*

# You've finished the book— now what?

Congratulations! You have just made the first step on your journey toward financial freedom. From creating a budget to setting financial goals and making an investment strategy, we hope this book has given you confidence and belief that you belong in the world of investing. Remember, you don't need a lot of money to start investing—the important thing is just to get started.

We hope this book has shown you that:
1.   You don't need a lot of money to begin investing.
2.   You don't have to be an expert to get started.
3.   Investing doesn't have to be time-consuming.
Spending just a little time learning about money management will give you time to do what you love later in life. You can cultivate your hobby, spend time with loved ones, or... just chill. And all while your money is working for you.

It is never too early to take control of your finances, nor is it ever too late. Remember, financial freedom is not a destination, it's a lifelong work in progress. It won't be perfect, and you'll experience bumps along the way, but rest assured, actively managing your money will be a game changer for your future, even if it's not the smoothest journey. You worked hard for your money. Now, it's time to let your money work for you.

# IT'S TIME TO CLAIM YOUR FUTURE

Investing is not about having a passion for financial markets. You don't think investing sounds interesting? That's fine. We're not here to have fun, we're here to make money and claim our well-deserved power; the power to make our own decisions and to own our future. We've said it many times throughout this book, but we'll say it once again: it's not about the money itself. It's about the freedom and independence it brings.

This might sound harsh, and it's very much intended to do so, because even though we've come a long way, we still live in a world where only 12 out of 195 countries offer full equal legal rights for men and women. Where the glass ceilings keep us from participating equally in business and politics, and where the right to make decisions that affect our own bodies is still up for debate. While we wait for the world to change, money is the only tool that guarantees us the right to truly make our own decisions.

You can't leave your financial future in the hands of others, because, trust us, no one will care as much about your money as you do. You worked for that money, you set your financial goals and you defined your values. Now it's time to put them into action. The good news? You can do it.

*Money is not a dirty word, it's a prerequisite for freedom and independence.*

# THE FINANCIAL FUTURE IS FEMALE

The timing for you to get started has never been better. Women are now being educated like never before, making money like never before, and challenging outdated stereotypes like never before. Now is the time to own our potential and break the biases. If we succeed, women have the potential to be the largest contributors of positive economic, social, and environmental change in the world. Think about it—what would the world look like if men and women were financially equal?

Generations of courageous women have paved the way for us, making sacrifices and leaving their comfort zones. Now it's our turn to keep up the momentum and get comfortable being uncomfortable when talking about money. This is not just a women's issue, and championing women to financially succeed should not just be done because it is the right thing to do; it should be done because when more women have more money, it benefits individuals, companies, and society as a whole.

There are no quick solutions to the problem of financial gender inequality, but while we wait for society to catch up and for governments to take action, we can take matters into our own hands by claiming our financial future and beginning to invest.

It's time for change.

Are you ready?

# GLOSSARY FOR NEW INVESTORS

**50/30/20 RULE:** When you split your budget into three different categories: 50% for necessities (housing, transportation, bills), 30% for fun (hobbies, dining out and holidays), and the last 20% for Future You (saving, high-interest debt and investing).

**AVALANCHE METHOD:** A method for paying off debt where you clear the debt carrying the highest interest rate first.

**BEAR MARKET:** When the stock market experiences prolonged price declines of 20% or more, which reflects pessimism amongst investors about the state of the economy. In turn, it causes investors to become nervous about their investments, who fear we're heading into a recession.

**BLOCKCHAIN:** A decentralized technology that powers most cryptocurrencies. Blockchain facilitates exchanges of information between people, such as payments, but without any middleman, like a bank. Blockchain technology uses an encryption technique called cryptography—which is very complex mathematical code—to secure the system.

**BONDS:** Represent a loan made by an investor to a borrower—typically a company or government. The borrower pays investors a fixed return rate for a fixed period of time. Unlike stocks, bonds don't give any ownership rights.

**BULL MARKET:** The opposite of a bear market, a bull market is an upward trend in prices and reflects optimism among investors around the state of the economy. It is an indication that economic expansion is on the way.

**CAPS:** Refer to market capitalization—in short, how "big" a company is. There are three types: small, mid- and large, all of which reflect the size of a company's capitalization.

**COMMODITIES:** Commodities are basic goods that can be transformed into other goods and services.

**COMPOUND INTEREST:** Much like a snowball effect, this is interest earned on money that was earned as interest. Also known as exponential growth.

**CROWDFUNDING:** When people—"the crowd"—are given the opportunity to invest in an unlisted company (not listed on a stock market), such as a startup. It allows businesses to turn community members into shareholders, who stand to profit should the business do well.

**CRYPTOCURRENCY:** Cryptocurrencies—or Crypto—are digital or virtual currencies that don't exist in any physical form but live only on a computer network. The most well-known cryptocurrency is Bitcoin.

**CURRENCY:** A generally accepted form of payment, typically issued by a government. Most countries have their own currency—such as the US dollar or the Japanese yen. Currency is crucial for facilitating trades across countries and works because every nation agrees that paper notes and coins have an inherent value, meaning we can use them to purchase goods.

**CYCLICAL/NON-CYCLICAL:** A term used to describe how a company (and hence a stock) is affected by development in the global economy. A cyclical stock will be more affected by the state of the economy, while non-cyclical stocks are less affected.

**DIVERSIFICATION:** The process of spreading out your risk in an attempt to combat market volatility, by investing in a range of different companies, across different regions, sectors, and countries.

**DIVIDEND:** A way of earning money through investing, where regular payments are made to shareholders out of the company's revenue, typically quarterly or annually.

**ETF:** Exchange-Traded Fund. A fund traded directly on the exchange. ETFs are different from other funds, as they are traded throughout the day. Made up of a variety of investments, including stocks, commodities, bonds, or a mixture of investment types.

**EXCHANGE:** Stocks are traded on an online stock exchange where companies and investors issue stocks to trade. Stocks are priced according to supply and demand. To trade stocks through the stock exchange, you need to access them through a trading app.

**FUND MANAGER:** Responsible for a fund's investment strategy and for managing its portfolio. A fund can be managed by one or two people, or by a team of many managers, depending on the size of the fund, and incurs a fee to do so.

**HYPERINFLATION:** Understood as an inflation rate that is above 50% during a given month.

**INDEX:** Used to track the performance of a certain type of stock, a specific sector, or a country's stock market. An example is the S&P 500 Index, which tracks the performance of the 500 largest companies listed on the US stock exchange.

**INFLATION:** This is the rate by which overall prices within an economy increase. Due to inflation, our money slowly loses value, which means you're losing purchasing power.

**INTEREST RATE:** When taking out a loan, the interest rate is the amount of money a lender receives for lending out money to you. This is typically expressed as an annual percentage rate (APR). When saving money, the interest rate applies to the amount earned at a bank from a savings account.

**IPO:** Initial Public Offering. When a company initially goes and makes stocks available to individual investors, who can proceed to buy stocks in the company.

**METAVERSE:** A virtual-reality space where users interact with a computer-generated environment and other users.

**MUTUAL FUNDS:** When a group of investors join forces and make mutual investments. They can be either actively or passively managed.

- **Actively managed mutual fund:** Has employees who analyse the market and choose a combination of investments based on expectations for the market in the future.

- **Passively managed mutual fund:** Follows the course of a certain index.

**NFT:** Non-Fungible Token. A term used in the crypto space. When you buy an NFT, you essentially get ownership of a digital item. NFTs are non-fungible, which means they are not interchangeable assets, because they are unique, have different characteristics, and therefore totally different values.

**P/E RATIO:** Price-to-Earnings value. Investors use this metric to decide if a stock is under- or overvalued and to evaluate the price of the stock compared to other companies in its industry. The P/E ratio is calculated by dividing the price per share by the company's earnings per share. For example, if a company's P/E ratio is 25, it means that its stocks are traded at 25 times its earnings. A high P/E does not always mean that a company is overvalued, and a low P/E does not always mean that a company is undervalued. The P/E should therefore not be the only thing you consider, but it can be a good indication of how attractive the stock is.

**PORTFOLIO:** Simply put, your portfolio refers to the basket of investments you own, across stocks, bonds, and investment funds. So if you own three stocks, your portfolio consists of three stocks.

**REIT:** Stands for "real estate investment trust." If you want to invest in property, but are not in a position to buy a full property yourself, then you can buy shares in REITs. These are companies that own and often operate a collection of properties—and any profits from rent, or increases in value, are shared among the shareholders.

**RETURN:** The money you accrue through investing. You can get returns in two ways: 1) when you sell a stock at a higher price than you bought it for, and 2) When you receive stock dividends, which is when a company decides to share benefits of its progress.

**RETURN ON INVESTMENT (ROI):** A term used to measure the success of an investment. It can also be used to compare the efficiency of an investment or a number of different investments.

**RISK APPETITE:** How happy you are to take risks with your money.

**SECURITIES:** Different types of financial assets that hold some kind of monetary value and can be traded. A stock is an example of a security.

**SHORTING:** Shorting (or short selling) is a trading strategy where an investor speculates on the decline in a stock or other security's price. When shorting, you essentially earn money when a stock decreases in value. Shorting has high risk and isn't considered a good strategy for less-experienced investors.

**SNOWBALL METHOD:** When you pay off the debt with the lowest balance first before you move on to the next, adding the amount paid toward the first debt onto that debt. This way, the amount you spend paying off debt will get bigger and bigger, like a snowball effect.

**STOCKS/SHARES:** Stocks represent ownership of a company. When you buy a stock, you own a share in the company. Companies issue stocks to investors as a way to raise money to fund growth, products, and other initiatives.

**STOP-LOSS/TRAILING STOP-LOSS:** Stop-loss is a tool provided by most trading platforms that ensures that your investment is automatically sold. Stop-loss comes in two different variations: stop-loss and trailing stop-loss.

- **Stop-loss:** Your investment is automatically sold once it hits a certain price decided by you.

- **Trailing stop-loss:** You decide a percentage decrease that will trigger the stop-loss to sell.

**TIME HORIZON:** A crucial factor to consider when investing. Your time horizon is the time you want to keep your investments. As a rule of thumb, you're a long-term investor if your time horizon is more than 5 years (or 10 or 30). A short time horizon is less than 5 years.

**TRADING ACCOUNT:** The main tool used by investors to invest. It offers access to stocks on the open exchange which you can buy and sell accordingly.

**VOLATILITY:** A term describing how stable a security or market is. When the price is relatively stable, the security has low volatility. If the security hits new highs and lows quickly or has dramatic increases and unexpected falls, the security has high volatility.

# REFERENCES

## Money is power

- Zakrzewski, A., Reeves, K. N., et al. (2020). Managing the Next Decade of Women's Wealth. www.bcg.com/publications/2020/managing-next-decade-women-wealth.
- Hutt, R. (2019). It Will Take 257 More Years to Close the Gender Pay Gap: Here's Why. World Economic Forum. www.weforum.org/agenda/2019/12/global-economic-gender-pay-gap-equality-women-parity-pay/.
- Madgavkar, A. et al. (2016). The Economic Benefits of Gender Parity. McKinsey Global Institute. www.mckinsey.com/mgi/overview/in-the-news/the-economic-benefits-of-gender-parity.
- Plan International. (2021). International Day of the Girl: 68% of UK Girls Feel Held Back by Harmful Gender Stereotypes. plan-uk.org/media-centre/international-day-of-the-girl-68-of-girls-feel-held-back-by-harmful-gender-stereotypes.
- UN City. (2022). Intersectional Feminism: What it Means and Why it Matters Right Now. un.dk/intersectional-feminism-what-it-means-and-why-it-matters-right-now/.
- International Labour Organization. (1995). Women Work More, But are Still Paid Less. www.ilo.org/global/about-the-ilo/newsroom/news/WCMS_008091/lang--en/index.htm.
- American Psychological Association. (2014). Girls Make Higher Grades Than Boys in All School Subjects, Analysis Finds. www.apa.org/news/press/releases/2014/04/girls-grades.
- Forbes. (2021). Data Shows Women Make Better Leaders. Who Cares? www.forbes.com/sites/avivahwittenbergcox/2021/03/06/data-shows-women-make-better-leaders-who-cares/?sh=1b39ce6746be.
- Taylor, L. (2017). Women in Developed Countries More Educated Than Men, But Still Earn Less: OECD. www.reuters.com/article/us-global-women-pay-idUSKCN1C911P.
- OECD. (2017). The Pursuit of Gender Equality: An Uphill Battle. OECD Publishing. 10.1787/9789264281318-en.
- Ojogbede, K. E. (2022). Female Investors in the UK. www.finder.com/uk/women-in-investing.
- Equileap. (2021). Gender Equality Global Report and Ranking. equileap.com/wp-content/uploads/2021/07/Equileap_Global_Report_2021.pdf.
- UBS. (2017). How Can Women Best Protect and Grow Their Wealth? www.ubs.com/global/en/wealth-management/insights/chief-investment-office/life-goals/2017/women-and-investing-how-women-can-best-protect-and-grow-their-wealth.html.
- Artz, B. et al. (2018). Research: Women Ask for Raises as Often as Men, But are Less Likely to Get Them. Harvard Business Review. hbr.org/2018/06/research-women-ask-for-raises-as-often-as-men-but-are-less-likely-to-get-them#:~:text=Women%20who%20asked%2obtained%20a,lifetime%20it%20really%20adds%20up.
- Bowles, H. R., Babcock, L., et al. (2007). Social Incentives for Gender Differences in the Propensity to Initiate Negotiations. Organizational Behavior and Human Decision Processes. 103 (1). 84-103. DOI:10.1016/j.obhdp.2006.09.001.
- Rodriguez, L. (2021). Unpaid Care Work: Everything You Need to Know. www.globalcitizen.org/en/content/womens-unpaid-care-work-everything-to-know/.
- PwC. (2017). Understanding the Unpaid Economy. www.pwc.com.au/australia-in-transition/publications/understanding-the-unpaid-economy-mar17.pdf.
- Clifford, C. (2020). Global Wealth Inequality is 'Founded on Sexism,' Says Oxfam International. www.cnbc.com/2020/01/17/global-wealth-inequality-is-founded-on-sexism-oxfam-international.html.
- AAUW. (2021). Deeper in Debt: Women and Student Loans. www.aauw.org/resources/research/deeper-in-debt/.
- Goodman, L., Zhu, J. et al. (2016). Women are Better Than Men at Paying Their Mortgage. Urban Institute. www.urban.org/research/publication/women-are-better-men-paying-their-mortgages.
- Matthews, C. (2016). Study Finds Women are Charged Higher Rates for Mortgages. fortune.com/2016/09/08/study-finds-women-are-charged-higher-rates-for-mortgages/.
- O'Callahan, T. (2020). Single Women Get Lower Returns from Housing Investments. insights.som.yale.edu/insights/single-women-get-lower-returns-from-housing-investments.
- Bucher-Koenen, T., Hackethal, A. et al. (2021). Gender Differences in Financial Advice. SAFE Working Paper. 309. doi:10.2139/ssrn.2572961 .
- Luxton, E. (2016). The Pocket Money Gender Gap - 12% and Growing. www.weforum.org/agenda/2016/06/the-pocket-money-gender-gap-12-and-growing/.
- Baker, N. (2021). Young Girls Do More Domestic Chores Than Boys, Study Finds. www.irishexaminer.com/news/arid-40322318.html.
- O'Reilly, C. and Quayle, M. (2021). Gender Inequalities in Time Spent Doing Housework by Children in Ireland: A Nationally Representative Sample Across Two Time Points. Infant and Child Development. 30 (5). 10.1002/icd.2246.
- Tinghög, G., Ahmed, A. et al. (2021). Gender Differences in Financial Literacy: The Role of Stereotype Threat. Journal of Economic Behavior and Organization. 192. 405-416. 10.1016/j.jebo.2021.10.015 .
- Giftcards.com. (2018). Adolescent Income and Financial Literacy. www.giftcards.com/adolescent-income-and-financial-literacy?utm_source=rakuten&utm_medium=affiliate&utm_campaign=2116208&utm_content=686295&ranMID=44432&ranEAID=TnL5HPStwNw&ranSiteID=TnL5HPStwNw-UYypwN6T4zEtjdln._pTgA.

- Vincent-Lancrin, S. (2008). The Reversal of Gender Inequalities in Higher Education: An On-going Trend. OECD Publishing. Higher Education to 2030. 1. Demography. 265-298. 10.1787/9789264040663-11-en.
- Backman, M. (2022). Women and Investing: 20 Years of Research and Statistics Summarized. www.fool.com/research/women-in-investing-research/.
- Davis, K. (2015). Has Gender Equality Stagnated in the Last 20 Years? www.fastcompany.com/3043438/has-gender-equality-progress-stagnated-in-the-last-20-years.
- Lalljee, J. and Hoff, M. (2021). All the Women on Earth Make About Half as Much Money as the Men. That's Barely Changed Since 1990. www.businessinsider.com/how-much-women-make-compared-men-wealth-changed-over-time-2021-12?r=US&IR=T.
- McKinsey and Company and LeanIn. (2021). Women in the Workplace. wiw-report.s3.amazonaws.com/Women_in_the_Workplace_2021.pdf.

## First... Prepare

- Berger, L. M. and Houle, J. N. (2016). Parental Debt and Children's Socioemotional Well-being. 137 (2). Pediatrics. 10.1542/peds.2015-3059.
- Fidelity Investments. (2015). Money FIT Women Study: Executive Summary. www.fidelity.com/bin-public/060_www_fidelity_com/documents/women-fit-money-study.pdf.
- Fidelity Investments. (2017). Fidelity Investments Survey Reveals Only Nine Percent of Women Think They Make Better Investors than Men, Despite Growing Evidence to the Contrary. newsroom.fidelity.com/press-releases/news-details/2017/Fidelity-Investments-Survey-Reveals-Only-Nine-Percent-of-Women-Think-They-Make-Better-Investors-than-Men-Despite-Growing-Evidence-to-the-Contrary/default.aspx.
- 7alış, Ş. (2018). 8 Steps For Growing Your Financial Confidence. www.forbes.com/sites/sherlyzalis/2018/06/16/women-money-8-steps-for-growing-your-financial-confidence/?sh=5f80f6502468.
- Science Daily (2019). How Happy Couples Argue: Focus on Solvable Issues First. www.sciencedaily.com/releases/2019/09/190916114014.htm.
- Rauer, A. et al (2019). What are the Marital Problems of Happy Couples? A Multimethod, Two-Sample Investigation. 59. Family process. 10.1111/famp.12483.
- Ramsey Solutions. (2018). Money Ruining Marriages in America: A Ramsey Solutions study. www.ramseysolutions.com/company/newsroom/releases/money-ruining-marriages-in-america.
- Little, S. (2018). Money Worries Biggest Reason for Marriages Ending, Survey Finds. www.independent.co.uk/news/business/news/money-marriage-end-divorce-day-relationships-personal-finances-slater-gordon-a8147921.html.
- UBS. (2021). UBS Own Your Worth report finds that only 20% of couples participate equally in financial decisions. www.ubs.com/global/en/media/display-page-ndp/en-20210506-own-your-worth.html.
- www.wiserwomen.org/nexphp?id%3D184&sa=D&source=docs&ust=1653054220712082&usg=AOvVaw1ldEF171NwzmgNJeS0Q1cg.

- UBS. (2019). Women Put Financial Security at Risk by Deferring Long-term Financial Decisions to Spouses, UBS Research Reveals. www.ubs.com/global/en/media/display-page-ndp/en-20190306-financial-security.html.
- Alliant International University. (2015). Professor Emeritus Dr. Robert-Jay Green on "Same-Sex Couples May Have More Egalitarian Relationships". www.alliant.edu/blog/professor-emeritus-dr-robert-jay-green-same-sex-couples-may-have-more-egalitarian.
- Brooks, R. (2016). Couples are happier when they talk about money. www.washingtonpost.com/news/get-there/wp/2016/09/19/couples-are-happier-when-they-talk-about-money/.
- Ramsey Solutions. (2018). The State of Finances in the American Household Survey. cdn.ramsey solutions.net/media/b2c/personalities/rachel/PR/MoneyMarriageAndCommunication.pdf.

## Next... Invest

- Voigt, K. and Benson, A. (2022). What Are Bonds and How Do They Work? www.nerdwallet.com/article/investing/what-is-a-bond.
- Female Invest. (2022). Bonds vs. stocks – what are the pros and cons? femaleinvest.com/magazine/bonds-vs-stocks.
- Michael, G. (2022). 3 Commodities to Invest in. www.investopedia.com/financial-edge/0412/the-3-best-commodities-to-invest-in.aspx.
- Fidelity Investments. (2021). Fidelity Investments' 2021 Women and Investing Study. www.fidelity.com/bin-public/060_www_fidelity_com/documents/about-fidelity/FidelityInvestmentsWomen&InvestingStudy2021.pdf.
- Birken, E. G. and Curry, B. (2021). Why Women Are Better Investors. www.forbes.com/advisor/investing/woman-better-investors/.
- Royal, J. and O'Shea, A. (2022). What Is The Average Stock Market Return. www.nerdwallet.com/article/investing/average-stock-market-return.
- SignalTrend Inc. (2019). S&P 500 Stock Market Index Historical Graph. www.forecast-chart.com/historical-sp-500.html.
- McDonagh, M. and Fitzsimons, L. (2021) Women Count 2021 Report. The Pipeline. vol. 6. execpipeline.com/wp-content/uploads/2021/07/Women-Count-2021-Report.pdf.
- Kollewe, J. (2021). Only Eight of UK's Top 100 Companies Headed by Women, Report Says. www.theguardian.com/business/2021/oct/07/only-eight-of-uks-top-100-companies-headed-by-women-report-says.
- Buchholz, K. (2022). How has the number of female CEOs in Fortune 500 companies changed over the last 20 years? www.weforum.org/agenda/2022/03/ceos-fortune-500-companies-female.
- Paytm Money. (2019). What are Mutual Funds? – Paytm Money Explains. medium.com/@paytmmoney/what-are-mutual-funds-paytm-money-explains-4ee9f395ef67.
- The Dow Jones Industrial Average Index. www.google.com/finance/quote/.DJI:INDEXDJX?sa=X&ved=2ahUKEwjZ3q6Q16X5AhWLTsAKHUx-rB-IQ3ecFegQIGRAY.

- The NYSE American Composite Index. www.google.com/finance/quote/XAX:INDEXNYSEGIS?sa=X&ved=2ahUKEwiak5Sp16X5AhVDiVwKHTh9Dj8Q3ecFegQIAxAY.
- Esposito, A. (2019). More Funds Run by Daves Than Women. www.morningstar.co.uk/uk/news/197122/more-funds-run-by-daves-than-women.aspx.
- The Core–Satellite Investment Strategy.
- Longo, T. (2021). Women's Biggest Financial Regrets: Not Investing More Tops List. www.fa-mag.com/news/women-s-biggest-financial-regrets--not-investing-more-tops-list-62375.html, Report by Bank of America, Merrill Lynch, Women & Financial Wellness: Beyond the Bottom Line.
- Lamont, D. (2020). The Data That Shows a Case for Long-Term Investing. www.schroders.com/en/uk/private-investor/insights/markets/the-data-that-shows-a-case-for-long-term-investing/.
- Zakrzewski, A., Reeves, K. N., et al. (2020) Managing the Next Decade of Women's Wealth. www.bcg.com/publications/2020/managing-next-decade-women-wealth.
- RBC Wealth Management. (2021). Women are Leading the Charge for Environmental, Social and Governance (ESG) investing in the U.S. amid growing demand for responsible investing solutions. www.rbcwealthmanagement.com/en-us/newsroom/2021-04-06/women-are-leading-the-charge-for-environmental-social-and-govern-ance-esg-investing-in-the-us-amid-growing-de-mand-for-responsible-investing-solutions.
- Curtis, C. (2021). The Future of Socially Responsible Investing is in Female Hands. www.cnbc.com/2021/11/10/op-ed-the-future-of-socially-responsible-investing-is-in-female-hands.html.
- The Morgan Stanley Institute for Sustainable Investing. (2019). Sustainable Reality: Analyzing Risk and Returns of Sustainable Funds. www.morganstanley.com/content/dam/msdotcom/ideas/sustainable-investing-offon-financial-performance-lowered-risk/Sustainable_Reality_Analyzing_Risk_and_Returns_of_Sustainable_Funds.pdf.
- Morningstar. (2022). Does Investing Sustainably Mean Sacrificing Return? www.librarydevelopment.group.shef.ac.uk/referencing/harvard.html#:~:text=Harvard%20style%20referencing%20is%20an,or%20bibliography%20at%20the%20end.
- Gupta, A. (2021). Top 5 Greenwashing Scandals of the Past Decade. www.jumpstartmag.com/top-5-greenwashing-scandals-of-the-past-decade/.
- Jacob, E. S. and Cáceres, E. S. (2022). Analysis of the Environmental, Social and Governance Information and Performance of European Airlines (from 2018 to 2020). reporterre.net/IMG/pdf/oscr_report_2022.pdf.
- Peel-Yates, V. (2021). Greenwashing: 10 recent stand-out examples. thesustainableagency.com/blog/greenwashing-examples/.
- Parla, L. (2021). 10 companies doing good for the earth. www.su.org/blog/10-companies-doing-good-for-the-earth.

- Adidas. (2019). Top Positions Achieved Again: Adidas in the Dow Jones Sustainability Indices for 20 Years. www.adidas-group.com/en/media/news-archive/press-releases/2019/adidas-dow-jones-sustainability-indices-20-years/.
- Beyond Meat. (2018). A Burger With Benefits: Beyond Meat Releases Impact Report Quantifying the Environmental Benefits of the Beyond Burger. investors.beyondmeat.com/news-releases/news-release-details/burger-benefits-beyond-meatr-releases-impact-report-quantifying/.
- Lucas, A. (2021). Chipotle will link executive compensation to environmental and diversity goals. www.cnbc.com/2021/03/04/chipotle-will-link-executive-compensation-to-environmental-and-diversity-goals.html.
- B Corporation Certification. www.bcorporation.net/en-us/certification.
- Fidelity. (2022). Fidelity's 2022 Money Moves Study. s2.q4cdn.com/997146844/files/doc_news/2022/03/Fidelity-2022-Money-Moves-Fact-Sheet.pdf.
- Ferri, R. (2012). Any Monkey Can Beat The Market. www.forbes.com/sites/rickferri/2012/12/20/any-monkey-can-beat-the-market/?sh=-617850c7630a.

## Now... Grow

- World Bank. (2022). Women, Business and the Law 2022. World Bank. vol.8. openknowledge.worldbank.org/handle/10986/36945.
- Buchholz, K. (2022). Only Twelve Countries Have Full Equal Rights for Women. www.statista.com/chart/17290/countries-with-most-equal-rights-for-women/.
- Elsesser, K. (2019). There Are More College-Educated Women Than Men In The Workforce, But Women Still Lag Behind Men In Pay. www.forbes.com/sites/kimelsesser/2019/07/02/now-theres-more-college-educated-women-than-men-in-workforce-but-women-still-lag-behind-men-in-pay/?sh=632b70844c31.
- Fund Selector Asia, (2022). Women's Wealth Growing Faster Than Men's. portfolio-adviser.com/womens-wealth-growing-faster-than-mens/.

All sources accessed April–May 2022.

# INDEX

# ABOUT THE AUTHORS

Have you ever had an a-ha moment? That's what happened when we (Emma, Camilla, and Anna-Sophie) met for the first time. We had all been investing since the age of 19, and we had all struggled to find the necessary information to get started. Most importantly, we all wanted to connect with like-minded women.

We quickly realized that our own search for women investors was a symptom of a global problem, heavily impacting the freedom and opportunities of women and marginalized communities around the world. We wanted to change this, so we launched an investment community called Female Invest, hosting educational events.

It started out as a passion project, but as the demand grew, we took the leap to become full-time entrepreneurs. We had no money, no network, and no experience. Taking the leap is the scariest thing we've ever done, the hardest thing we've ever done, and, without comparison, the most meaningful and exciting thing we've ever done.

Today, we're called Rebelle Invest. The name has changed, but the mission to close the financial gender gap hasn't. We've built an online educational platform used by women and non-binary people in 80+ countries with more than 100,000 individuals taking our courses. We are deeply passionate about financial empowerment, and we're not done until everyone has the same opportunities to understand and manage money.

At the time of writing, we've raised $7 million in funding, and every dollar has been invested in empowering our community. Why are we sharing this? Because these numbers show that financially empowering women and non-binary people is not just a moment, it's a movement.

The journey has only just begun, and we can't wait to bring you along. Are you ready?

**Senior Acquisitions Editor** Zara Anvari
**Senior Designer** Tania Da Silva Gomes
**Project Editor** Kiron Gill
**Editor** Helena Caldon
**US Editors** Susan Hobbs, Lori Hand
**Designer** Andy Warren
**Editorial Assistant** Charlotte Beauchamp
**DTP Designer** Heather Blagden
**Proofreader** John Friend
**Indexer** Hilary Bird
**Jackets Coordinator** Jasmin Lennie
**Production Editor** David Almond
**Senior Production Controller** Luca Bazzoli
**Editorial Manager** Ruth O'Rourke
**Design Manager** Marianne Markham
**Editorial Director** Cara Armstrong
**Art Director** Maxine Pedliham
**Publishing Director** Katie Cowan

First American Edition, 2022
Published in the United States by DK Publishing
1745 Broadway, 20th Floor, New York, NY 10019

Copyright © 2022 Dorling Kindersley Limited
DK, a Division of Penguin Random House LLC
23 24 25 26   10 9 8 7 6 5 4 3 2
009–334483–Dec/2022

Text copyright © 2022
Camilla Falkenberg, Emma Due Bitz, Anna-Sophie Hartvigsen

A catalog record for this book
is available from the Library of Congress.
ISBN: 978-0-7440-7730-8

Printed and bound in Slovakia

**For the curious**
www.dk.com